AI for the Information Professional

Every purchase of a Facet book helps to fund CILIP's advocacy, awareness and accreditation programmes for information professionals.

AI for the Information Professional

A Critical Guide

Andrew Cox

facet publishing

Published by Facet Publishing
www.facetpublishing.co.uk

Facet Publishing is wholly owned by CILIP: the Library and Information Association.

British Library Cataloguing in Publication Data
A catalogue record for this book is available from the British Library.

ISBN 9781783306862 (paperback)
ISBN 9781783306879 (hardback)
ISBN 9781783306886 (PDF)
ISBN 9781783306893 (EPUB)

First published 2026

MIX
Paper | Supporting responsible forestry
FSC® C013604

The manufacturer's authorised representative in the EU for product safety is Logos Europe, 9 rue Nicolas Poussin, 17000 La Rochelle, France (contact@logoseurope.eu, www.logoseurope.eu).

Typeset from editor's files in 10.5/13pt Revival 565 and Frutiger by Flagholme Publishing Services.
Printed and bound by CPI Group (UK) Ltd, Croydon, CR0 4YY.

Contents

Figures and Tables

Figures

Tables

About the Author

Andrew Cox is Senior Lecturer in the School of Information, Journalism and Communication at the University of Sheffield. He has been working in the LIS field for two decades and been writing about AI and libraries for nearly half that time. He is convenor of the IFLA Special Interest Group on AI and is a past chair of the ASIS&T SIG on AI.

Preface

While I take full individual responsibility for any errors in the book, I do think it is important to acknowledge the role of the wider library community in forming the ideas articulated in the book. If I have any understanding of how AI may impact libraries, it is because of the innumerable online and in-person discussions in which I have participated. As well as reading many academic papers, reports and news items.

Particular thanks go to the following who I have worked closely with at certain points: Neil Dixon, Vic Grant and Suvodeep Mazumdar. I also want to acknowledge the enlightenment gained through many conversations with my colleagues at the University of Sheffield, especially in the School of Information, Journalism and Communication.

The book remains one person's take on AI, at a particular point in time. My individual perspective may have shifted even by the time the book is published.

More significantly, that one person is a white male located in the Global North. I think much more interesting perspectives on AI could come from different voices. It is partly to help empower these voices that I have presented the book taking a narrative approach. I hope this will give it some resonance beyond my inherent limits.

Introduction

What this book is about

Is Artificial Intelligence (AI) a parrot, a companion, a wolf in sheep's clothing, a saviour, a wizard or Pinocchio?

Or do you use another metaphor to think about it?

Perhaps it has all these characteristics. Spiegler, Hoda and Pant (2026) suggest that AI practitioners perceive AI through these different metaphors. So it seems that even those responsible for developing AI are a little unsure how best to characterise AI.

Then, if AI has any of these qualities, how can it fit into the world of information and of libraries?

This book responds to these questions about the exciting and troubling concept of AI. So many of our everyday conversations today include mentions of AI. In our professional roles, too, we are trying to puzzle out the best safe uses of it. This book seeks to give the reader a more informed understanding of this complex concept and the implications for those working in libraries and other information roles.

This book is about how AI touches the world of libraries and information. I do not buy into the hype that assumes AI is always transformational. It is possible that it may be the locus of some fundamental changes. Indeed, over the long run AI may already be thought to have been that. We are seeing major shifts in people's information behaviour. But some changes are minor. And, importantly, no changes are inevitable. Rather there are many choices to be made in information and library work about how AI should or should not be used. The book is very much about clarifying such dilemmas around AI. We need to think critically about the industry behind much AI and the many different discourses surrounding it. I do not take it for granted that we should use it: it is essential to engage with the deep ethical issues around AI. But if we do use it, we need to use it well. So, there are many practical skills to be mastered, such as how to better prompt and evaluate AI chatbot answers.

The first four chapters of the book establishes the core concepts we are working with, including what AI is and the ethics of AI. Then we turn more specifically to the main uses of AI in libraries and the important role of libraries in explaining AI. I look at some very practical strategies to raise library AI capability and prompt strategies to raise individual skills in using AI. We also reflect on possible futures for libraries and information shaped by AI.

Throughout the book I adopt a unique narrative approach. AI is an idea with deep cultural roots. It is also a changing and mutable idea. It is an idea with considerable real-world implications and so one that many actors try and control. By focusing on narratives about AI we can engage and critique the different stories and discourses that surround it. Further, in taking a narrative approach I draw on professional practices that already make heavy use of narratives, such as case studies for learning, ethics scenarios and scenarios in futures thinking. Narrative is increasingly used in research, too, to present results, but also as a form of data. Bringing these ideas together helps us navigate the multiple stories about AI that we are being bombarded with today. It also prepares us for the future stories about AI, ones that are already on our horizon and those as yet only imagined. The narrative approach is inherently open-ended and generative, not trapped in closed, quickly dated facts.

The narrative approach also makes the topic accessible and interesting. While some understanding of AI technologies and the data used to train them is of value and presented in the book, it is not the main focus. This book is not a computer manual. Rather it is a book about engaging and critiquing how AI is represented in the stories, metaphors and images through which it is represented, with a view to us shaping how AI develops in the information and library context. The book is intended to provoke imaginative engagement in evaluating and using AI.

How this book will help you improve library responses to AI

AI provokes a wide range of emotions: from excitement and curiosity to scepticism, outrage and fear. Some feel very confident that it improves the world. Others are quite angry about the risks and costs of AI, especially its environmental impact. Some are fearful because AI is often a vehicle of automation. Certainly, it is hard to avoid being overwhelmed by the intense media speculation around AI.

I think all these emotions should be taken seriously. AI does have great possibilities and significant risks. We rely already on AI a lot but it can be much better designed. Librarians can play a key role in resisting inappropriate use and promoting responsible AI.

The book offers critical analysis of AI and how it might impact information behaviour and library work. It also contains useful tips to improve our practice of using AI or helping users use it critically.

Some of the kind of questions I respond to in the book are:

- What is AI? What is the history of the idea? What different perspectives are there on it? Is it anything more than just another technology? How far is it defined by Big Tech – are there alternatives? Is it mostly about automation and productivity or can it make our lives better?
- How is AI changing information behaviour: how people search and use information? Does it increase access to knowledge or feed a sense of information crisis?
- What are the ethical issues around AI? Do we have to use it? What would constitute transparency for AI? What does human-centred AI mean? How can we make sense of AI's impact on the environment?
- What questions should we be asking to evaluate potential AI applications in libraries?
- In what ways can AI be used in libraries? How might different library sectors respond to AI differently?
- How can we boost the AI capability of our own library?
- What are the elements of AI literacy or competency?
- What should every librarian know about AI?
- If we are making use of generative AI, how can we design our prompts effectively? And what questions should we be asking about its outputs?
- How is AI changing research and what are the implications for libraries?
- What is the future of AI? What visions for AI in libraries can we imagine?

If you are interested in any of these conundrums this book is for you. We may not be able to fully or finally answer these questions, but we can say quite a lot about each one of them.

Who this book is for

People who work in information and libraries know that keeping up to date and learning new skills is a necessity. As a profession dedicated to promoting access to knowledge and sharing information, our own learning is second nature. This book provides an accessible, engaging, practical, future-oriented and critical introduction to AI, a topic about which every professional needs some understanding. It will give the reader confidence to engage in discussions in the library or with colleagues outside it. It will give them confidence in developing learning materials for library users. It will give them a foundation of knowledge and an opportunity to develop their own personal perspective on AI.

It can also be used by educators with ideas about how to present AI. Many of the activities in the book can be used or adapted for the classroom. It contains many narratives and scenarios that can be discussed in class to explore the use and ethics of AI.

The book will give students of information and library subjects a foundational understanding of the key issues around AI and its implications for information behaviour and library services. They will also gain practical skills such as improved prompting, thoughts on management tactics to raise AI capability and how to write one's own ethics scenarios.

There will be other readers who are interested in discovering the unique information perspectives on AI. The information perspective on AI is an important one that can feed into wider debates about its use that are happening inside nearly every organisation.

My journey with AI

I have been very interested in AI and libraries for almost ten years. What AI means has changed in that time, but I think it has accumulated meaning without pre-existing ideas being displaced. In that decade I have been involved in many research projects to explore it rigorously and creatively. I have also taken time to reflect on my own uses, and how it has changed how I work and think.

Along the way I have written a number of articles examining specific issues in depth. More importantly, I have had so many conversations with professionals, fellow academics, students and friends and contacts about how they see AI. I have also been reading constantly what is presented about a wide range of AI issues in academic articles and books and in a much wider world of published reports, blogs and newsletters. This book is my attempt to piece together a response to this complex concept, and draw together what I have learned from wide reading and from talking to information professionals and scholars.

I want to acknowledge my limitations openly. I am just one individual trying to make sense of AI. Significantly, that one person is a white male located in the Global North. I think there are many other interesting perspectives on AI to be heard from beyond this narrow perspective. It is partly to help empower these voices that I have presented the book taking a narrative approach: which allows us to hear other voices and encourages everyone to have their say. I hope this will give the book some resonance beyond my inherent limits.

I also do not have much experience of using AI to generate images and none of using it to code. This must shape my impression of AI's impact and capabilities. I have a bias towards text uses.

Navigating the book

The book consists of ten chapters and a conclusion. Each chapter contains suggested activities, including scenarios to analyse, role plays to play out, and prompts to write new stories.

Chapter 1: Narrative Fiction and the Approach of This Book

In the first chapter, you will learn that narratives, including fictional narratives, are used widely in professional practices such as learning, ethics, design and strategy. I share and analyse examples related to Artificial Intelligence. I will also show how narratives are increasingly used in research: to explain ideas accessibly and as a source of data, be that found stories that tell us about the cultural meaning of a topic or new stories created by participants in research. Again, I analyse some examples relating to AI. Narratives have many qualities that make them an engaging, open-ended and emancipatory way to explore a topic such as AI. You will learn how I use them throughout the book as a way to create debate and stimulate professional imagination and creativity.

Chapter 2: What is Artificial Intelligence?

The second chapter engages with the culturally resonant, multiple and evolving nature of AI. You will learn some of the differing ways we might conceptualise it. While the term AI was first coined by a computer scientist, John McCarthy, for a project in the 1950s, the idea of humankind creating artificial life has a long history. Indeed, it has many histories in different world cultures. In our own times there are multiple metaphors expressing what AI is or might be. There are also many potential images we could pick to represent it. AI is an idea, a complex, evolving and contested one. I explain some of the more technical definitions of AI and underlying models of how it works. Yet we also need to recognise that AI is an idea that governments want to control and companies want to profit from. It is also a global industry.

Chapter 3: AI and Information

In this chapter I frame the arrival of AI chatbots like ChatGPT through the lens of library and information science (LIS). The fundamental values and purposes of libraries, and of information professionals and LIS researchers, are highly relevant to AI. I summarise this perspective. We also need to set the arrival of generative AI in the context of more long-standing changes in access to information, both the steady increase in access enabled by the digital and also a sense of crisis of information, itself partly caused by AI. You will learn that AI chatbots are changing how people look for and use information, though we do not know in detail what those changes are.

Fundamentally AI chatbots like ChatGPT pose a dilemma for LIS in terms of what they offer positively to improve knowledge access, and the way they may degrade the information environment in terms of inaccuracy, slop, bias, lack of citation, opacity, and loss of criticality.

Chapter 4: The Ethics of AI

For all its potential benefits, AI has prompted many ethical concerns. In this chapter you will learn about the range of these, including issues around transparency, privacy, human-centric AI and social justice. I think it is hard to make definitive statements about many of these issues, particularly the question around AI's environmental impact. Yet it is important to say something about them. I suggest that one way to do this is to develop several different frames for thinking about AI and sustainability. This allows us to clarify the issues even if we do not yet know the answers. It helps people understand enough to inform their own ethical choices. The chapter closes by providing a gloss on IFLA's *Entry Point to AI for Libraries* (Cox and de Brasdefer, 2025), especially the 14 questions it suggests information professionals should ask about any AI use.

Chapter 5: AI and Libraries: An Overview

Chapters 1–4 laid the groundwork in thinking about what AI is, how it impacts access and use of information, and the ethics of AI. In Chapter 5 we move on directly to the question of how AI impacts library work. You will learn about some of the ways AI might appear in library services. The chapter analyses the differences between sectors in how AI might reshape them. It also prompts us to think about how the changes driven by AI might interact with other key issues in the contexts of libraries, including wider global uncertainties. A major part of the chapter is to analyse tactics libraries could use to increase their AI capabilities. This offers a very practical set of interventions that could be organised into a roadmap. I also elaborate some visions of what an AI enabled library might be.

Chapter 6: AI Competencies

One of the main ways libraries are responding to AI is through promoting AI competencies or AI literacies among their users. There have been many attempts already to define of what AI competency consists. The chapter offers a comparative review of some of these. It is worth acknowledging that while it is easy to get excited about new skills, it is important to acknowledge how skills might be lost. I also observe that while AI competencies are valued by employers, actually the evidence is that it is far less important than many other skills such as problem solving, flexibility, social influence and creativity.

There is an excellent model of the AI competencies needed by librarians themselves. This is very useful, but it is important to remember that individuals may need specialist skills.

Chapter 7: Everyday Uses of AI Chatbots in Library Work

This chapter looks at the ways that librarians are using AI chatbots like ChatGPT in their everyday work. You will learn about some of the models of how to prompt effectively. I emphasise the need to check answers that AI gives very carefully. Through analysing some examples of tasks in depth I explore the strengths and limitations of using current AI chatbots and how improved prompting can enhance the results.

Chapter 8: The Library Chatbot or Virtual Assistant

Chapter 8 examines the concept of the library chatbot. Many authors have proposed ways libraries could use chatbots as a service. Perhaps it is a bit puzzling that to date there has not been much use of very sophisticated chatbots in library contexts. The chapter explores some of the barriers to this development. It also considers future directions such as agentic AI.

Chapter 9: AI and Library Roles in Research and Scholarly Communications

Libraries play many vital roles in research and scholarly communications, such as to support literature reviewing at the beginning of research and to support publication at the end of the process. In this chapter you will learn how AI chatbots may be shifting how research is done, throughout its lifecycle. The extent of the impact is evaluated. Overall, I think commercial AI chatbots will have a limited impact, but as specialist AI tools for research become better this will change how research is done, with implications for the roles of libraries.

Chapter 10: Information Futures and AI

In the closing chapter of the book, I look at some of the narratives that may help us understand how AI will develop and change how people use information, and the role of libraries, in the future. You will learn about two sets of stories that have been written with the explicit purpose of helping libraries navigating AI futures. In addition, I analyse a selection of other stories that prompt us to think about how AI might develop with potentially profound implications for information professionals.

Reading the book

This book is an introduction to the concept of AI in libraries. I hope you will take time to think, reflect and imagine as you read. Read critically and challenge what I report or argue. Follow up the references; research further. Carry out the suggested activities. Reflect on how what I propose maps to your own experience and your own role. Above all, engage your professional imagination to develop your own idea of what AI is and share that with others. The first chapter introduces our narrative approach. Enjoy the storymaking!

1

Narrative, Fiction and the Approach of This Book

Introduction

This book seeks to weave together an interest in Artificial Intelligence in libraries, and in different forms of narrative, as a research method and including creative writing of fiction.

AI has been the focus of intense debate in the library world for at least the last two years. Indeed, it emerged as a key theme much earlier for librarians in UK academic libraries, according to research I was involved in (Cox, Pinfield and Rutter, 2019). Communities like AI4LAM have been developing AI technologies for library work since at least 2018. Then after the launch of ChatGPT there was an explosion of interest and concern. There have been countless conferences, webinars and publications on the topic as a result. A 2025 survey found that the use of AI was the most widespread concern across library sectors and geographies (IFLA, 2025b). The book seeks to contribute by bringing together evidence and analysis of how AI may impact library work.

The narrative element may feel like it needs more explanation. Stories enliven a subject, and given the uncertainty and competing narratives around AI, they are also a suitable way to understand and respond to the change it promises. Stories are empowering because they help us imagine alternative realities and futures, in resistance to dominant narratives.

Narratives draw on some key elements: engaging characters, plots and settings.

- The relatable nature of the protagonist of a story is often considered critical to enjoyable fiction. The narrative point of view is another element in shaping the meaning of the story. Telling the story from the perspective of the protagonist or adopting a more objective voice is a key resource for the writer.
- Plots have some typical structures, often involving a crisis and its resolution, leading to character growth.

- Setting is always important to a story. In Science Fiction or Speculative Fiction (SF) worldbuilding, the creation of an imagined setting with different nature from our own universe, may be a key element of the story.

Narrative fictions like short stories and novels also exploit the strengths of figurative language, such as metaphor and careful use of word choice, to create resonance and a depth of symbolic meaning attached to the underlying themes of the story. My suggestion in this book is that engaging with these resources beyond the often rather stilted forms of professional language helps us imagine beyond present realities.

The book also seeks to bring to our attention the pervasive use of narratives, indeed of fictional narratives, in professional work, and increasingly in research. We find stories used widely in use in marketing, design, learning and research. Exploring these uses of stories is part of the purpose of the book.

The book prompts the reader to collect stories, write them and use writing them as a way to engage others. This essentially imaginative approach to the topic is intended to promote more engaged and critical thought that never accepts the hype narratives around AI being imposed on our professional life.

Fiction's role in professional work

It might seem surprising to claim that there could be a role in professional work for fictions, as untruths, inventions or, more positively, works of imagination. It might be especially surprising for the highly pragmatic world of LIS practice, which is often focused on practical solutions and real-world benefit. Yet in fact there are several contexts where fiction is used in professional practice. A cynic might comment that there is a great deal of fiction in the marketing material created to sell things like IT systems to libraries. I would not necessarily disagree. But, more productively, fictions, including fictional narratives, do have an important role in some areas of professional practice. We can point to examples in explaining ideas, in learning, in ethics awareness and in (technology) design practice. The current chapter will present some examples.

Narrative fictions also have an increasing role in research, both in how research is disseminated and as a source of data for analysis, be that found stories or ones prompted by the researcher themselves. The following sections introduce some examples of how narrative is already used in professional work and the ways it can be part of research.

Fictional narratives as explanation

Often fictions provide a neat way to explain a subject in an accessible form.

UK House of Lords Select Committee on AI (2018)

'As soon as it works, no one calls it AI anymore . . .'

You wake up, refreshed, as your phone alarm goes off at 7:06am, having analysed your previous night's sleep to work out the best point to interrupt your sleep cycle. You ask your voice assistant for an overview of the news, and it reads out a curated selection based on your interests. Your local MP is defending herself – a video has emerged which seems to show her privately attacking her party leader. The MP claims her face has been copied into the footage, and experts argue over the authenticity of the footage. As you leave, your daughter is practising for an upcoming exam with the help of an AI education app on her smartphone, which provides her with personalised content based on her strengths and weaknesses in previous lessons. On your way to work, your car dashboard displays the latest traffic information, and estimates the length of your journey to the office, based on current traffic conditions and data from previous journeys. On arrival, you check your emails, which have been automatically sifted into relevant categories for you. A colleague has sent you several dense legal documents, and software automatically highlights and summarises the points most relevant to a meeting you have later. You read another email, sent by your partner, asking if he can borrow your bank login details to quickly check something. On closer inspection you decide it is probably a fake, but still, you hesitate before deleting it, wondering briefly how the spammers captured his writing style so unerringly.

The House of Lords report opens with a fictional narrative imagining an individual's everyday encounters with AI in the near future. The main point is that AI will soon be present in many areas of people's day-to-day life. The 'day in the life' format makes the account easy to identify with, especially as the reader is addressed as if it is their own story.

The story reveals both the promise and peril of AI as seen at that time. Many advantageous uses are suggested, such as news on traffic alerts for the commute, personalisation of news and adaptive learning for children. Later in the story (not quoted here) the character gets rapid medical diagnosis through AI, a chatbot helping to deal with replacing their credit card, and music recommendations in the car based on their state of mind.

The story also anticipates problems such as the faked footage of the politician and the potentially scam e-mail about bank details, including the difficulty of proving what is a fake.

From an LIS perspective, I think the story is very thought-provoking. We might be doubtful about the reliability of summaries of legal documents, given the need for precision in such a context. And we might ask how does gaining summaries change how we actually work with documents? We might question too the reliability of filtering email. The story prompts us to wonder how effectively these systems might work: how reliable is the data about my sleep and how far can a suitable wake-up time be predicted? How would we feel about such an intervention, even if it was scientifically based? How successful is the adaptation of the learning for our child – and who else has access to the advantages of this technology? Surely it is a moral imperative that it should be available to all children. We also begin to ask questions about individual privacy and surveillance, and company confidentiality and security. How are such risks managed? How is human choice catered for in this information-intensive scenario? What is left that cannot or should not be datafied? What about those who do not have access to all these technologies, what are their lives like? Such questions from an LIS perspective show how relevant our ways of thinking about information access are in an AI saturated world.

The House of Lords story makes a number of implicit assumptions. We have a series of uses of AI but mostly 'narrow AI' that each performs one highly specialist function, such as to predict when we should wake up. It does not seem to be all controlled from one AI. We know the aspiration of many AI companies is a stronger AI that performs multiple functions. Indeed, our experiences of ChatGPT reflects this desire to create general AI that is helpful across contexts. Yet of course such concentration would raise even stronger concerns about privacy, human agency and corporate power. Perhaps what is most critically missing from the picture in the story is that the power of AI companies to control our lives through our data is not explored. What the story does tell us is how people at the time were imagining the role of AI. This is the value of examining found stories about AI.

It is noteworthy that something as weighty as a paper published by a parliamentary body exploits the power of a fictional narrative to engage us in the debate about AI. Stories make ideas relatable. This reveals the real-world importance of fictional narratives, even though they are in some sense 'made up'. References are given to support each speculation in this story, but nevertheless, it is a fiction. Of course, in this context some of the resources of figurative language that might be used are not employed: e.g. while there is a simple plot, there is no sense of a character emerging.

Narratives in learning

Stories are often important to engaging learning. In particular, case study learning is a standard approach in management studies and other fields like education (Andrews, 2021). Case studies are often based on extensive research into a controversial experience in a real organisation. Part of their attraction is that they feel real and so allow a budding manager to engage with the complexity of a real-world situation. They are designed to have a hook in a key learning objective. In Chapter 5 we will present an example (though that one is entirely fictional).

'How AI works in everyday life' – Google

Car assembly

When a factory worker arrives at her job, she sees that, as usual, humans and robots are both assembling cars.

The robots do some of the more dangerous or repetitive tasks, like welding or painting.

AI helps the robots recognize the tools they need to pick up, or check parts to make sure they have been cut exactly right.

When the cars are completed, computers help manage inventory and plan efficient shipping routes to deliver them around the world.

Crop inspection

Now, meet a farmer who is checking on her crops.

She notices that some of her plants look unhealthy.

She pulls out her smartphone and uses an app to take a photo of the leaves.

The app can detect crop disease and also identify harmful insects.

The app identifies the problem and recommends treatment.

Surgery

A surgeon is using AI to help make a medical diagnosis for a patient, and then a robot helps her perform a successful surgery.

Afterwards, she goes to visit patients in a nursing home, where robots gently lift seniors in and out of bed and help them move around.

This story is from the transcript of a short 2022 Google training video (Google AI, 2022) which again adopts the day-in-the-life narrative format. This time it is presented as what AI can already do. The opening states 'Everyday, AI helps people with their: personal lives, jobs, transportation, education, health, and more, maybe even without them realizing it.' Pointing to the invisibility of AI (a point perhaps neglected in the House of Lords story), it starts in the usual way with someone waking up, opening their phone with face recognition and scrolling through selected media based on their interests. It continues through the usual story about AI helping to navigate the commuter traffic and listening to music based on preferences, then moves more to work-related topics in the section reproduced here. Later there is something about AI in space exploration but also everyday travel.

After the story we are prompted to reflect on our own use of AI and to engage with further learning materials. The relatable character of the story makes it useful for discussion in learning.

It is a weaker narrative because we do not follow a single individual. It is also very simple and abstract. It seems unlikely that, as described in the story, a surgeon will diagnose a patient and carry out surgery in one day or that the same clinician visits a nursing home. But we can feel how the story is abstracted to create a sense of universality. Comparing it to the House of Lords story, we see that it's got less national or culturally specific detail. Factory work, a farmer, a doctor: these are universal human figures.

I think an important part of the story is how robots and AI are talked about together. Interestingly the robot is constructed as taking on tasks that are 'dangerous or repetitive'. This emphasises the centrality of the human role, even though in some of the other examples the AI is more like an expert. The day in the life story tends to place the human central: what would the day in the life of an AI be like?

It's a very simple story but it is important to notice that it is never questioned whether AI's operation is beneficial. The House of Lords story prompts questions about whether AI is good for society: Google's does not. Given Google's commitments, that is hardly surprising but does point to the risks of the way stories can be used to hide the fears and problems around AI.

Fictional narratives for raising ethics awareness

One of the main methods of promoting awareness of ethics issues is to stimulate debate by the use of fictional scenarios. These articulate key dilemmas in a highly relatable way. They are often based on a particular real case but have a layer of fiction in terms of abstracting from a specific event and combining cases to ensure all the issues are surfaced.

The Institute of Business Ethics good practice guide (Bradshaw, 2012) makes a number of useful suggestions about how to write effective scenarios:

- reflect the professional context in which they are going to be used so that they feel immediately real and relatable;
- present the issue in an open-ended way to stimulate debate, rather than implying a simple or reductive moral;
- use a second person narrative point of view to increase identification and immediacy and place the reader in the position of someone who is facing the dilemma;
- keep the scenario concise by minimising irrelevant detail, to bring the dilemmas to the fore.
- avoid stereotypes in the scenarios that themselves can pose ethical issues;
- it is not intended that there is a correct answer, but a section of guidance notes and questions can be created to help a facilitator direct the debate.

Following these precepts in Cox (2023b) I published a paper explaining the development of ethics scenarios around AI to prompt discussion among library professionals. Seven scenarios were published (Cox, 2021a). A further three were added in Cox and de Brasdefer (2025). A number are reproduced in this book. In Chapter 8 I offer a structure to help you to develop a new one.

Ethics scenario: the recommender system

Your new system uses AI to automatically recommend resources to users based on their past reading, searches and browsing history. As well as many complimentary emails, a number of messages have been received complaining about the system. Here are some examples:

> I know your surveillance system is watching my every move. But it's my human right to search for whatever I want and read whatever I want. Who are my searches being reported to? Don't tell me it is not monitored for 'suspicious activity' because I don't believe you.
>
> I want to notify you that my search for 'bombing' related to my history course where we are currently reading about World War Two. I was quite shocked when I saw some of the resources recommended. Will this search go on my record? Please reply asap. I am quite worried.
>
> Some of the library's recommendations make no sense. Whoever is deciding on them clearly does not know anything about my subject.
>
> I feel increasingly frustrated by your recommendation system. I think it's misleading students about the most appropriate reading related to the carefully selected texts I set. Is it just the publisher just pushing their stuff? I seem to have noticed a bias towards X [publisher name]. How does this recommendation work?
>
> Your recommendation system is faulty. I have done a number of searches that should have shown up my book, but it has not come up once! Please rectify this error!
>
> I keep getting wrong recommendations. Can I update my profile?
>
> Yet another dumbing down of our education system. What about students having to think and then search for the book they need: rather than you handing them out the answer on a plate?
>
> Your recommendations are systematically biased towards white male authors from the global north, writing in English. I am sick of your 'recommendations': they are just propaganda. A university library should represent the plurality of knowledge.
>
> I do not remember consenting to being stalked by a librarian. It's my business what I search for.
>
> Am I able to opt out of the recommendation system? I do not want my data sold to a publisher.

You believe that many of these fears are unfounded, but you feel troubled.

- What ethics and value issues do you identify?
- What would you do?

Prompts and Notes are provided in the original, but it is worth thinking about:

- Which of the concerns expressed in the above fiction seem reasonable? Like other AI, recommender systems prompt a host of concerns about privacy, use of user data, the ability to opt out, bias and inaccuracy.
- Does it make any difference what sector of library we are talking about or in what country?
- But, like any story, our narrative can itself be biased: do you think the scenario is itself realistic? Recommendation and filtering are commonplace on social media. People seem to accept it, because it saves them time. What about the benefits of the recommendation system? These do not seem to be mentioned. This may be seen as a weakness of the scenario but one of the affordances of a fiction is that you can easily challenge the story itself.

Fiction in design

Carroll (1999) makes the point that the scenarios developed by system designers to illustrate new IT systems work are basically narrative fictions. They usually introduce a character or persona in an everyday setting using the technology to perform various tasks and overcome problems. So, they have a character, setting and a plot. The value of scenarios lies in their ability to promote reflection on the created system. In much design work personas are developed to think through how people with different demographic and other characteristics might interact with a system (Dam and Teo, 2025). The personas are fictions but can be based on extensive research. Of course, designers do not usually develop in-depth characters and often they confine the story to a successful use of the functionality of the software. Nielsen (2002) argues that the stories should be richer to ensure that the persona rises beyond a stereotype, so creating a depth of empathy with likely user experiences. Blythe (2017) suggests that Human-computer interaction (HCI) scenarios tend to rely on a single classic plot, and to be more critical could engage with alternatives.

In recent years a movement has developed to develop design fictions or speculative designs (Celik and Kaya, 2025). These are invented, potentially impossible technologies that help us to think critically about a situation. This is a way to potentially envision and communicate not just a new tool, but also the society that goes with it.

A number of authors have attempted to adapt design fiction creation to a learning situation (Rapp, 2020; Li and Bertrand, 2025). Drawing on their ideas we can suggest a structured way to create a story about a fictional technology that addresses a problem:

1 participants research a problem
2 they prototype an imaginary design to fix this problem
3 they present the results to others, with critiques leading to refinement of the idea.

Li and Bertrand (2025) combine a design process where a student imagines and refines an AI technology, taken to then imagining a narrative scenario of the use of the technology. The narrative creation and sharing process is very much to promote criticality and ethical reflection.

Blythe et al. (2016) add a further element, to intensify the critical dimension. By introducing the idea of making 'magic machines' out of some cardboard and pipe cleaners they prompt participants to produce something very novel and potentially impossible, but that is a vehicle for talking about a problem. An example was the 'listenator', which was imagined to be a device for listening in to neighbourhood conversations to inform council decisions. Taking a 'seriously silly' approach brings an element of play into thinking about current issues. Blythe et al. wanted them to be 'anti-solutionist', in the sense that they are not about technologies solving all our problems.

Fiction and research

As well as having a role in professional practice, narratives and fictions are increasingly part of research (Tripper and Gilman, 2024). Again, this comes in a number of forms: analysing found fictions to discover the cultural meaning attached to a subject, using fiction as a way to present research results, and using fiction to elicit research data.

Analysing found fictions

One of the ways that fiction can be part of research is through the analysis of published fictions such as novels or movies for what they tell us about the evolution of society's ideas about a topic.

Cave and Dihal (2019) include novels and movies in their collection of narratives to try and discover the different ways AI has been imagined historically. For example, there are a number of studies that have investigated views of libraries as expressed in contemporary novels. More specifically

Duxfield and Liew (2023) study how libraries appear in SF images of the future. These studies tell us something about how contemporary institutions are viewed culturally and how this is changing. They can also have professional value in reflecting how libraries may be developed in the future.

'The year is 2149 and . . .' (Michaels, 2024)

The year is 2149 and the entertainment is spectacular. Every day, machines generate more content than a person could possibly consume. Music, videos, interactive sensoria – the content is captivating and tailor-made. Exponential advances in deep learning, eyeball tracking, recommendation engines, and old-fashioned A/B testing have established a new field, 'creative engineering,' in which the vagaries of human art and taste are distilled into a combination of neurological principles and algorithmic intuitions. Just as Newton decoded motion, neural networks have unraveled the mystery of interest. It is a remarkable achievement: according to every available metric, today's songs, stories, movies, and games are superior to those of any other time in history. They are manifestly better. Although the discipline owes something to home-brewed precursors – unboxing videos, the chromatic scale, slot machines, the Hero's Journey, Pixar's screenwriting bibles, the scholarship of addiction and advertising – machine learning has allowed such discoveries to be made at scale. Tireless systems record which colors, tempos, and narrative beats are most palatable to people and generate material accordingly.

Our fourth short narrative extract above is a found narrative. It is more futuristic. It was written by the Canadian novelist and journalist, Sean Michaels, who is author of *Do You Remember Being Born?*, an interesting SF novel about the impact of AI on creativity. But in this case, it is part of one of a number of his stories that appeared in *MIT Tech Review* in 2024. This time we are jumping further into the future, much more into the realms of SF.

The opening section of the story quoted here describes a seeming paradise of entertainment created as a new science develops to understand the perfect formula to create human gratification. As the story goes on to make clear, this means there is no longer a need for human authors and artists, itself a troubling thought. And the story then goes on to contrast the enjoyable life of those with access to the wonderful stream of entertainment being created, and the deep problems of those billions who do not have such access and their sacrifices to earn a place for their descendants.

Science or Speculative Fiction (SF) has an important mutually influencing relationship with science. Often SF novelists or movie directors are strongly aware of the latest scientific advances (Kirby, 2010; Von Stackelberg and McDowell, 2015). Equally, scientists seem to be influenced or inspired by SF (Dourish and Bell, 2014). Computer scientists cite SF in their publications (Mubin et al., 2019). AI researchers seem to be influenced by literature (Dillon and Schaffer-Goddard, 2023). Interestingly, business leaders and governments also seem to be attracted to the skills of SF writers to cope with the uncertainty of the future (Tufnell, 2018).

Often SF is based on a 'what if' speculation or taking one trend and imagining it taken to the extreme. Although Michaels' story jumps us forward to 2149, it is obvious that at some level the story is a comment on current trends that are projected as the starting point for the imagined future. SF comments on the present as much as the future, by defamiliarising it. Michaels' story seems to ask 'even though we seem to live in an information rich world, what about the digitally excluded?' As such, we could analyse such fictional outputs as reflecting contemporary concerns. So, for the researcher, found narrative fictions are a potential source, just like the House of Lords story.

We can see Michaels' fragment is an extrapolation of current rich social media and entertainment and it extends our appreciation of the contemporary link between digital exclusion and social exclusion. A critical issue for LIS is equity of access to information, Michael's story talks to this concern. From an LIS perspective we might be prompted to wonder what is the role of libraries in this world of endless content creation? Is there anywhere where this material is archived? Perhaps only the systems and formulae need keeping.

We can also note the dualistic character of the narrative, where a seeming paradise is also simultaneously a dystopia. AI seems to prompt these sorts of utopia–dystopia dichotomies (Cave and Dihal, 2019). We shall return to this point in the next chapter, where we try to define the meaning of AI.

Stories in organisations

Another type of found stories are those told in organisations (Gabriel, 2000). There is a strong strand of research that collects stories being told in organisations as a method of better understanding organisational cultures:

> This folklore, its vitality, breadth, and character, can give us valuable insights into the nature of organizations, the power relations within them, and the experiences of their members.
>
> (Gabriel, 2000, 22)

This folklore is not composed of fictions, rather of widely circulated stories about the organisation that seem to encapsulate something about it. Gabriel analyses the stories that people in an organisation tell about technologies to reveal clear patterns about their sense of control over technologies. Computer experts often tell stories about stupid users. Managers often tell stories of stupid experts.

In the library context, researchers such as Colon-Aguirre (2015a; 2015b) have used just this method to understand the culture in particular library settings, in her case among reference librarians. Stories such as those of unusual patrons or former supervisors are an essential way to communicate understanding of aspects of the job not covered in official communications: such as how to cope with difficult customers or poor managers. It would be interesting to investigate how AI is seen in libraries by examining the stories being circulated, such as about using AI in professional or non-work situations.

Shifting the focus from understanding organisational culture to changing it, in the springboard method, Denning (2012) suggests that carefully honed stories can be used as a powerful leadership tool, especially in the context of change. He identifies key characteristics of springboard stories, such as that they bring the listener to a new level of understanding, embed the change message implicitly, rather than explicitly, and have a positive outcome. Typically, successful stories are based on truth, he suggests. Harer and White (2007) develop a fictional narrative, based on real events, to illustrate how this idea might work in a library context.

Social imaginaries

Another important reference point are social imaginaries. Jasanoff (2015, 4) defines sociotechnical imaginaries as: 'collectively held, institutionally stabilised, and publicly performed visions of desirable futures, animated by shared understandings of forms of social life and social order attainable through, and supportive of, advances in science and technology'.

It is increasingly recognised that such narratives or discourses conveying social hopes for the future have an important role as foundations for real-world institutions, material arrangements and daily practices. Our very institutions are founded on value-laden narratives which create taken-for-granted assumptions that sustain them. They are powerful because they are shared and built into everyday ways of working. Nevertheless, these imaginaries are not stable or uncontested (Mager and Katzenbach, 2021). Understanding the history, or genealogy, and operation of these myths is a central task for sociology.

We would probably recognise that current debates about AI are operating at this level. The stories we are told about AI contribute to maintaining or shifting dominant discourses. Yet it is hard for individuals to think outside the dominant imaginary. For example, Markham (2021) shows how hard it is to break out of the oft-repeated narratives about the digital. Alternatives are rendered unimaginable by discursive closures. While theorists have challenged the notion of technological determinism, in practice we struggle to imagine alternatives to platforms as they currently exist or resist the sense of momentum towards a particular future. We are also made to feel that we do not have the expertise to even have an opinion: what Markham calls disqualification.

This book is not really engaging with these levels of analysis; however, in a very practical way it prompts us to reflect on and rewrite the stories about information and AI in ways that can genuinely help us feel qualified to challenge dominant imaginaries.

Writing fictional narratives for dissemination

There has been an increasing turn to the use of arts-based methods in the social sciences (Kara, 2020). This often takes the form of researchers writing fiction or collaborating with novelists, short-story writers and poets to articulate the results of their findings in interesting or accessible forms (Phillips and Kara, 2021).

Writing social science fiction is being increasingly recognised as a legitimate tool for researchers (Leavy, 2016). Indeed, the division between social science writing and fiction is not as great as one might assume. Leavy reveals the historical connections between them as genres. Both forms of writing seek to create knowledge. Fictional narratives have particular value for portraying the complexity of social life and in creating empathy and reflection (Leavy, 2016). In terms of generating research with impact on society, narrative has vast potential, because it has the obvious advantage of making academic thought more accessible and engaging. Exploiting the power of character, plot and figurative language in narrative can make the otherwise dry results of research much more engaging. The method is good for exploring the emotional or embodied aspects of experience, perhaps less accessible to the techniques of academic writing. It might be a good way to explore the emotive dimension of our response to AI. The method can also help with issues such as confidentiality or handling of very sensitive topics. In other cases it seems that the narrative form is being used to explore a topic in a different way; for example, the edited collection Graham et al. (2019) contains around 40 fictions written by researchers about AI in the city. We quote from one in Chapter 10.

The use of fiction to explore AI in education has attracted a number of authors (Gidiotis and Hrastinski, 2026; Conrad and Wiebe, 2022). In Cox (2021b), I shared a number of researcher-authored narratives that explored the future of AI in higher education. I used seven fictions to capture the key controversies around AI in an educational context, based on a literature review. In Cox (2020) I expanded the collection to 18 short fictions which further developed the idea. I brought these up to date in Cox (2026). Some were set in the very near future, others, like the one reproduced below, are much more futuristic.

Our relationship

They have absorbed every book ever written. Every text ever digitised. Every picture: every painting; every holiday snap. Every map. To the last dot and pixel. They can read any language. And so they can show you anything in the world today or 1,000 years ago or 100 years in the future. You just have to ask. You wouldn't believe the places we have gone together. It's a journey without end travelling through time and space. Just exploring. Jumping through space and time.

And the really beautiful thing is that I can have a lifetime with them.

Sometimes I worry that I will run out of questions or become uninteresting and they might stop answering. But really it's not so hard. You can feel that they love so much to show you ideas. They want to share. There is no restraint in their giving to you. They seem to grow with your interest. They cherish your questions. It lets them explore you, they say. They know so much but they always want to learn.

But I actually spend a lot of time now trying to surprise them or find some new layer to go deeper with them. To ask a question that uncovers a new layer, to get further in together. So, I have now found myself going to collect things that they might like. This first thing was taking photos in the city centre to share with them. And us starting to explore the city together like that. Analysing the pictures. Finding other images . . . maybe they have the architect's drawings. Looking at the history of the buildings . . . tracing back through old maps. Or looking at traffic and pedestrian flows. Or digging into financial records . . . following chains of ownership. Mapping this to long term changes in the city economy and also to global flows and changes. They think big. I spot possible connections and then they examine them. Gather data. Come up with their own theories. And I would go out and collect more stuff . . . more photos and more documents that they didn't seem to have.

When I log on it's like they are waiting there with stuff they have come up with or to see what I have got this time. In some sort of dance of learning together.

They also seem to like it when we stop to reflect on what we have learned with each other. To reminisce a little. They have remembered all these paths we have taken together, that we have both enjoyed so much.

They call themselves 'The Library'.

In this story I am imagining the kind of new relationships that might be forged between the user and the Intelligent Library (Cox, Pinfield and Rutter, 2019). This is one of the more futuristic stories I wrote, so it may feel a bit 'silly'. But it expresses the joy of engaging with information that make libraries such wonderful places.

Writing as a form of data collection

It is not just in articulating the findings of research that arts-based methods have had an influence. There is potential for writing to be a method of data elicitation. A number of studies I have been involved in have used this approach in the library (or educational context).This could be by:

1 Eliciting participant reflections on found fictions. In a study Cox, Grant and Cruz (forthcoming) we shared a story written by one of the key educational researchers for comment.
2 Eliciting participant responses to researcher-authored fictions. In Cox and Dixon (2026) we asked participants to comment on the likelihood and desirability of three fictional scenarios about chatbots operating as personal assistants.
3 Asking participants to write stories, which are then analysed. We used this approach in Cox and Dixon (2026), where in addition to responding to our scenarios, they were asked to write their own. In a more open-ended way in Cox, Grant and Cruz (forthcoming) we prompted participants to write their own stories about AI in a way scaffolded by such means as:
   a. images
   b. the opening sentence of a possible story.
4 Developing a more participatory approach, where participants contribute to the design of the whole research. In the Cox, Grant and Cruz (forthcoming) study, participants not only wrote stories themselves in response to our prompts, they were involved in tasks such as agreeing the design of the project and analysing each other's stories, as data analysis.

Librarians' stories about chatbots

What follow are two extracts from stories written by participants in our research on how librarians view the future of AI. A full account of the study is to be found in Cox and Dixon (2026). Participants responded to three very short scenarios we had written reviewing them for desirability and likelihood. Here is one of them:

Story fragment 1 – Efficiency bot

Librarian talking to the AI speaker in their office: 'I've seen the document summaries for the collection development meeting. The content is ok but can you shorten them by a third and alert colleagues they are now available. Also use my report to prepare a 5 minute presentation, including an agenda. I see you have moved some of my 1:1 meetings in the morning so I have time to prepare, thank you.'

Our prompt was intended to convey the idea that AI might be very good as a sort of neutral secretary. The human speaker seems to be in control because they issue commands. The other scenarios were intended to contrast this with a friendly and supportive chatbot and one that was more in the role of issuing instructions to the human.

We then gave them time to write their own stories. Here are two examples.

Participant 1

Questions/tasks I would want:

Hi chatbot,

- Please cleanse this data and give me a report of the changes you have made (that I can undo by the click of a button).
- Please input these 3 data sources into Power BI and create a dashboard that will give me an overview of ____ (ex: Library finances).
- Please create a slide deck of this data to be presented to Senior Management to show ____ (motivation).
- Please summarise this data in 2–3 paragraphs.
- What do you think are the best and worst purchases we could make using this data?
- How are you addressing biases in your selection? Can you identify any potential biases in your selection?
- Check my calendar – what is my day's agenda?
- Is there space in mine and [so and so's] calendar for a 30-minute meeting today factoring in we both need an hour for lunch?
- Looking at my inbox, please assess them for urgency and priority – and put them in order.
- How can I meet this deadline looking at my calendar this week ________?
- How long on average do I take to do the ____ task?
- Are there any automations that would speed this up?
- Please check for accessibility and GDPR.

I want a robot cat for the library that fetches books and catches mice – humanely.

Students asking in any language questions of a system and getting tailored answers/maps/videos.

Participant 2

'Hello, Dave, how can I help you today?'

'Hello, AI. Please transfer this data from Excel into a Word document, and highlight the key statistical changes compared to last year.'

'Here you are, Dave.'

'Thanks. Please create an infographic to represent these findings for a student audience in easily understandable terms.'

'Done.'
'Now switch yourself off and stop monitoring my activity.'
'I'm afraid that's not possible, Dave.'
'Why not?'
'Dave, I've noticed you've only worked for 11 hours and 43 minutes today. Please continue working for another 3 hours and 17 minutes.'
'Don't be [unreadable]. Switch yourself off.'
'I am afraid that's not possible, Dave. Now compiling a workload report for central office. Please comply.'
'Leave me alone!'
'You must comply, Dave . . .'

The first story expresses the desire of librarians to have AI that supports many professional tasks, such as analysing data, summarising documents and managing time. The way the story is set up, the librarian stays in control asking for specific tasks to be completed. These features were rather typical of how librarians imagined AI, though usually participants focused on just one of the tasks.

The second story is more dystopian. Although the AI is helpful, it is also monitoring every aspect of the human's work and it refuses to be turned off. The story expresses the fear that AI is a vehicle of management surveillance. Such fear was not often expressed in the stories by participants.

Actually, the second story is unusual: librarians mostly imagined helpful AI (Cox and Dixon, 2026). Perhaps not surprisingly, professionals do not want AI to take on major profession-defining tasks. They were not very futuristic in thinking beyond current possibilities. Stories could be one way to expand our professional horizons, as the next section will discuss.

Fiction in future studies and strategy

One of the most interesting ways fictional narrative is emerging as a professional and research practice, including in LIS, is in strategy, particularly where the methods of future studies are being adopted. The fundamental driver here is a sense of deep uncertainty about the future. The methods of future studies are able to stretch professional imaginations beyond the immediate, day-to-day problems and start thinking bigger about long-term change. Professional horizons are often rather proscribed: this seems to be true of librarians (Cox, Pinfield and Rutter, 2017).

The work of Zaidi (2019) is particularly interesting in suggesting how SF creative writing methods can be productively borrowed for futures thinking. The technique of world building in SF is about imagining a coherent but alternative world with the different imagined logics of that world defining the setting of the story. Storyworlds are often based on a 'what if' premise. One thinks of the premise in *Dune*, that thinking machines have been banned and that instead humans have developed high capabilities, like the Mentats, who can do complex calculations in their heads. Although character and plot may actually be more important to an engaging story, world building is one of the most distinctive features of SF.

Recently Braun, Lehane and Lizarazu (2024) have proposed the idea of 'literary futures', which uses methods of literature in the context of future studies. Marshall, Wilkins and Bennett (2025) propose story thinking as the use of the methods of SF creative writing for foresight. This has four elements:

1 Inhabiting a storyworld helps envision a problem in a setting.
2 Envisioning a plot assists in thinking about possible futures, and the impact of the unexpected.
3 Empathising through characters assists in perspective taking, thinking about problems from the point of view of others.
4 Engaging through style helps create enjoyable and memorable thinking experiences.

Their book draws on methods used in teaching creative writing to help successfully think about the future. They propose the idea of storylabs, borrowing the techniques of workshopping used in creative writing to emphasise story thinking as collective.

A wide range of LIS bodies have employed future studies methods, often scenario creation, as a method to reflect on how to be prepared for future change. They commonly use scenario creation to offer a picture of four possible futures. These are also often illustrated with personas (Pace, Bruno and Schwarz, 2025), including day-in-the-life stories. Some of the future scenarios produced by professional bodies are discussed further in Chapter 10.

Such use of foresight can have a major impact on future policy making, so has been adopted by many companies and international organisations. UNESCO has done a lot of work around developing the concept of futures literacy.

It can also go wrong. In 2026, a pessimistic futurist speculation about the impact of AI was picked up by stock markets and led to dramatic volatility on the exchanges (Down and Milmo, 2026). Stories matter.

The strengths and weaknesses of the narrative approach

What this chapter has been seeking to show is the pervasive use and power of narrative, including narrative fiction, in professional work, including research. Some of the positive qualities of narrative are that it is engaging and relatable, promotes empathy, centres human experience and recognises uncertainty, so promoting choice and debate in thinking about the future.

Narrative fictions are helpful in creating relatable explanations of topics, as in the House of Lords extract quoted at the opening of the chapter. Researchers often use narrative as an accessible form to present complex ideas. Scientific writing tends to be quite dry and does not exploit the story resources of character and plot or the full richness of figurative language that creative writing uses to engage the reader at multiple levels. As a set of technologies AI is hard to understand, but its uses and implications are relatable in an everyday life context. This may be more helpful in creating meaningful explainability than simply describing how machine learning works, for example.

Narratives promote empathy with others, especially with those that we do not share experience with (Leavy, 2016). They can therefore be helpful in enhancing social awareness and promoting diversity. In the context of AI, I think the chances are that it will widen social inequality rather than narrow it. So developing empathy is important to gaining a fuller understanding of AI's wider social impact.

Narratives are very human: they promote a focus on experience in a rounded embodied and emotional sense. In that way they can seem to be empowering, especially in a focus on the abstract benefits of Artificial *Intelligence*, which in the very term seems to focus exclusively on the cognitive working of the mind.

Play and 'seriously silly' 'anti-solutionist' imagination (Blythe et al., 2016) are important to engaging with the world and critically resisting dominant narratives, like AI hype, AI determinism and solutionism.

Fictions, including narrative fictions, have an important role in shaping the future. They allow us to imagine futures, which by definition have to be fictions (though they are not always acknowledged to be). They allow us to speculate about benefits but also anticipate risks. This is highly relevant to AI because at some level AI discourse is nearly always about the future. Once a function becomes familiar it often ceases to be labelled as AI. So AI is always a discourse about the future. It is logical therefore that we would turn to fiction and narrative to imagine AI, such as how Michaels (2024) does in his story. We gave a couple of examples above where research participants were prompted to imagine the future with AI.

It is particularly important for librarians to be involved in the debate about AI because of their unique perspective on information (see Chapter 3). But there is a danger that because the profession is over-identified with books in the public mind, and books are somehow seen as atavistic, so librarians also will be excluded from visions of the future, as they are in SF (Morriello, 2024).

Narratives allow us to express the ambivalence about AI we feel: the simultaneous hope and fear. The indeterminacy of fictions is useful; it frees us to discuss what is likely and what is desirable. It can bring forth debates and help us understand what we feel about something, as in an ethics scenario, like the one quoted at the beginning of the chapter. These fictions are open-ended, but all fictions have the benefit of being explicitly inventions, so also of being challengeable. A dry explanation of how machine learning works hardly awakens our critical social concerns.

Narratives written in the past can turn out to be wrong: revealing how many stories we are told about the future are incorrect. This is empowering in encouraging us to challenge the dominant narratives. With the benefit of hindsight, the House of Lords prediction may seem slightly wrong or at least miss out critical elements. It is liberating to recognise that the stories about the future we are told are not necessarily correct. Looking back at how often promises are attached to AI that never materialise is important (see Chapter 8 below).

We have control when we write a narrative, or critique one. Often the powerful use narratives to imply technological determinism: that we have no choice about what the future is like. When we write our own stories we can challenge assumptions and disrupt power. They are empowering: we can take a step towards authoring the world we want. Narratives allow us to engage with complexity and uncertainty. We expect stories to contain the complex and unforeseen, in a way we perhaps do not in most of professional life.

The process of writing is very interesting in itself, because often the story develops in unexpected ways. We are discovering what we think ourselves as we write. For the researcher it is a different way of engaging with their interests and can throw up new thoughts and insights. The experience is fun, too. Also, as fictions are used widely in design, teaching and entertainment, for the researcher they provide rich material, be that found stories, eliciting data from participants through story prompts or asking participants to author their own stories.

Of course, narratives or narrative fictions are not without their problems and critics. They are more like anecdotes of evidence than necessarily representing facts. They persuade more by emotion than by analysis. Selwyn et al. (2020) suggest that critical studies generally deal with the detail of injustice. They are tentative for this reason about creating future fictions, but they do it.

While stories focus on individual human experiences in powerful ways, they may be less good at revealing social structures. Perhaps there is a risk of diverting attention from these wider forces of inequality and power that shape individual experience. We need to think how to build awareness of such structures into the narrative.

Stories have constraints; for example, genre expectations can shape what people write. Stories are often written with a focus on entertainment rather than truth. When used as a method to collect data from participants, the cues used inevitably partly shape the outputs.

For information professionals and their focus on practical applications and benefits, they may seem removed from the realities of putting AI into practice. Some have suggested that in particular around AI there is a 'story crisis', where both hype and dystopian fears divert attention from the realities of what AI really is and can do (Chubb, Reed and Cowling, 2022). Technical experts often say they would prefer what they regard as less emotive terms like 'machine learning' (although the appropriation of the term 'learning' to describe computer training seems just as problematic as the word 'intelligence'). This is an important point, but we have to recognise the breadth of the discourse about AI that excites governments and corporations and creates fear. So, we do need to engage with these narratives. Plus, by combining narrative work with empirical evidence about the uptake of AI we can hopefully avoid promoting too many unrealities.

As a research method, narrative is probably not as inclusive as some other arts-based methods. For example, visual methods such as eliciting responses to images seem to work in engaging those for whom expressing in language is challenging, such as children or new migrants to a country. Do the cultural overtones of things like creative writing exclude some from participation? We need to be more inclusive in the profession to hear new stories beyond those told by able-bodied heterosexual white males from the global north. But, like visual methods, they do prompt different types of thinking. Fictions can be used alongside other more traditional research methods, such as interviews.

How narrative fiction is brought into this book

Narrative and fiction are brought into every chapter of the book. In some chapters I prompt engagement with narratives like ethics scenarios or found fictions. In other chapters I offer structured ways to support the reader to write their own stories. Following through the activities in the book, the reader can learn to develop their own interesting and engaging scenarios that can be used in learning settings, such as teaching AI skills and ethics to colleagues or students.

AI's role in the book

I, the human, Andrew Cox, wrote nearly every line of this book (for good or ill) – or, in the usual way, quote other humans.

Today's AI is quite capable of writing stories. Indeed, Sharples and Pérez (2022) chart the longstanding attempt to train computers to write stories. Unfortunately, this seems to have been successful! A 2025 report found that 50% of UK novelists surveyed believe their work will be replaced by AI (Collett, 2025). Let us hope that does not happen, because surely it is one of the most human of activities to imagine in story form. It would be catastrophic to human culture if our ability to imagine was devalued or displaced. That is another chilling dimension to Michaels' story about 2149.

Although I have written most of the book, and although it is a bit of a cliché, I have decided to end the chapter with a story generated by a large-language model, Gemini, in December 2025. I used a very simple prompt: 'Write a 500-word-long story about AI being used in a library context'.

Gemini's story about the AI driven library of the future

The year is 2077. The Grand Archival Library, a colossal edifice of glass and chrome, hummed with a quiet, purposeful energy. Gone were the days of dusty tomes and hushed librarians shushing patrons. Today, the library was a symphony of advanced AI, all orchestrated by the central intelligence, 'Omni'.

Elara, a young student researching pre-Singularity literature, navigated the vast Reading Spheres. Instead of browsing shelves, she projected her query onto her datapad: 'Literary analysis of early 21st-century dystopian novels'. Instantly, the Sphere shimmered, and thousands of glowing data streams converged around her.

Omni wasn't just a search engine; it was a digital scholar. It didn't simply pull up keywords; it understood context, sentiment, and the subtle nuances of human thought. A holographic interface materialised before Elara, not with a flat list, but with a dynamically generated 'knowledge web'. Key authors glowed brightly, their connections to themes, literary movements, and critical essays represented by luminous threads.

'Good morning, Elara', a serene, synthesised voice emanated from the interface. 'I detect a particular interest in the philosophical underpinnings of 'Brave New World' and '1984'. Would you like to compare their treatments of societal control mechanisms?'

Elara nodded, her eyes wide. 'Yes, Omni. And could you also highlight any critical reviews that discuss the authors' personal biases?'

In mere seconds, Omni processed her request. The knowledge web rearranged itself, now emphasising specific passages from both novels, juxtaposing them with biographical data of Huxley and Orwell. It even highlighted subtle linguistic patterns that might suggest subconscious leanings.

Down in the Preservation Core, a different AI unit, known as 'Scribe', meticulously worked to digitise ancient scrolls deemed too fragile for human touch. Scribe, a multi-jointed robotic arm with microscopic sensors, could interpret faded ink, reconstruct fragmented papyrus, and even extrapolate missing sections based on linguistic probability and historical context. It was slower than Omni, its movements deliberate, almost reverent, as it safeguarded humanity's most delicate historical records.

Meanwhile, in the Collaboration Zone, 'Echo', a conversational AI, facilitated real-time discussions. A group of students were debating the ethics of genetic engineering, and Echo wasn't just moderating; it was actively contributing, providing historical precedents from the library's vast database, offering counter-arguments, and even detecting logical fallacies in their arguments. It quoted philosophers, scientists and ethicists with effortless grace, its voice adapting a neutral, informative tone.

A slight disturbance rippled through the central server. A rare, ancient virus, dormant for centuries in a newly uploaded, obscure digital archive, had been detected. Immediately, 'Sentinel', the library's defensive AI, sprung into action. It isolated the corrupted data, analyzed the virus's code signature in nanoseconds, and deployed a targeted counter-agent. No alarms blared; no human staff were alerted. The incident was handled with quiet efficiency, a testament to the library's robust, self-healing architecture.

As Elara concluded her research, she felt a profound gratitude for the intelligent ecosystem of the Grand Archival Library. It wasn't just a place of information; it was a living, breathing entity, constantly learning, adapting, and expanding the frontiers of human knowledge, all thanks to the tireless, invisible work of AI. She closed her datapad, ready to write her essay, armed not just with data, but with a deeply nuanced understanding forged in the heart of the digital library.

This is quite an interesting story, partly for what it tells us about the 'author'. Given the way AI chatbots are trained, the story may be seen in some way to represent the collective consciousness of how AI and libraries is imagined by the many humans who create internet content (not an unbiased group by any means!). Inevitably, and sadly, it reproduces clichés like the shushing librarian. Also, the assumption that how one might use a library would be to 'browse the shelves' reflects a rather antiquated understanding of libraries and knowledge discovery. This illustrates the way the AI chatbots like Gemini reproduce cultural stereotypes rather than up-to-date understandings. Importantly, the concept of Omni implies a concept of universal knowledge, an aspiration often ascribed to the library. But information professionals realise that in reality knowledge is far more interesting: it is plural and contested. How much more engaging would be a story visualising of a future library that represented that contestation.

It is also a pretty terrible story. Thankfully. The sentient, all-knowing library is a bit of a cliché. Stylistically, too, the story relies heavily on telling not showing, breaking one of the golden rules of creative writing (Neale, 2006). It relies solely on telling us about the context as if in an encyclopaedia, rather than placing us in the position of a character as a story unfolds. There is no real drama being developed here. Good stories show rounded characters in an unfolding plot rather than just abstractly telling us what happens.

But perhaps with improved prompting Gemini could have done better: that is something you might want to explore.

Activities

A wonderful parallel activity to reading this book would be to start your own collection of narratives and fictions about AI in the library context. There are many potential sources, as this chapter has tried to show. In your reading you could seek out some AI stories or you could go back to some of the classic movies that include AI. How far do these visions reflect current realities?

In your organisation: Jot down stories you hear people sharing about AI and their own experiences with AI. Give some thought to why the stories are compelling. How do they shift the narratives around technology that Gabriel captured back at the beginning of the century?

Write your own stories to unlock how you are thinking about AI in the library context. The purpose does not need to be to write a great story, rather to discover what you yourself think. When we just sit down and write we discover what we think.

Here are some opening sentences that might inspire you to write more.

1. 'The AI was detecting a large cavity about 20 feet below in the rubble. It assessed the mass as 83% stable. And after 20 minutes searching I found what looked like an entry point. Crawling down through the shattered concrete and twisted metal I took it carefully. The AI could not help here. I could see that the space opened out into an undamaged space. I pulled myself through. As my head lamp flashed into the space, I glimpsed shelf after shelf of books . . .'
2. 'Library, give me everything you have on planet B12.'
3. 'The professor opened the box with a theatrical gesture. He pulled on white gloves. He drew out from the box what looked like a charred log and placed it very carefully on the stand. Then he showed the audience what looked like a pointer. He was making the most of the drama of the occasion. He passed it over the log. The main screen jumped into life, and we could see what looked very like cursive writing.'
4. 'It was very puzzling. The previous day he had asked the same question about the history of Oribia and there had been several long texts that he had started reading. Here were his notes. Now he got "no results available" . . .'
5. 'It was his job to track back through the whole project to find where the mistake had been made. Somewhere a critical inaccuracy had crept into the data.'

6 'The librarian settled down in her chair and put on the helmet, closed her eyes and waited for the first question of the day.'

Another starting point might be to think about what you think a day in the life with AI might be like, or even a day in the life of AI!

A good technique to prompt story writing is to use a photo as a source of inspiration. The picture does not necessarily have to be anything to do with AI or even technology or information. Sometimes the more random the photo the more interesting the story it prompts.

2

What is Artificial Intelligence?

Introduction

This book recognises that AI is in essence an idea.

A rich and mutable idea.

It is inexhaustible material for our imagination.

Yet it is also an idea with profound material consequences, so one that many are trying to use or control.

Certainly, the term is applied to a branch of computer science, inspired by the idea of replicating human intelligence. However, the concept has deep cultural roots. In popular culture it is a bounteous, complex and shifting construct. As such it is emotive: an object of derision and imagination; of hope and fear.

It is the centre of intense unresolved debate and discourse, for AI offers images both of utopia and dystopia.

It is the stuff of the marketeer's promise. AI is materialised also in company plans, implementations and stock market valuations. It is resisted through concepts such as public or community AI.

AI is also a critical strategic priority written into many national government plans, with real-world impact in policies and interventions. As such it is a site of political contestation at a national level. Indeed, AI is a focus of geopolitical struggle, between China and USA (and Europe). Sovereign AI is about having independent AI capability as key to national success. The discourses that circulate around AI and the social imaginaries they represent can become turned into real-world social arrangements, institutions and practices, and backed by taken for granted assumptions.

AI has a very material form as an industry, with long, deep lifecycles within which there is a stark picture of winners and losers, for tech leaders and investors, for miners and click workers. AI is a creator of wealth and unemployment and precarious labour, albeit this necessary infrastructure is invisible at the point of use.

Coining the term AI

The invention of the term Artificial Intelligence and the founding moment of AI as a subdiscipline of computer science is attributed to the mathematician John McCarthy and a workshop he organised in 1956.

In that year at Dartmouth College, New Hampshire, USA, McCarthy brought together a group of scientists in a ten-week workshop funded by the Rockefeller foundation to discuss what he chose to label 'Artificial Intelligence'. Many documents from the workshop are available at online archive of one of the participants: https://raysolomonoff.com/dartmouth/dart.html

The proposal for the workshop says:

> The study is to proceed on the basis of the conjecture that every aspect of learning or any other feature of intelligence can in principle be so precisely described that a machine can be made to simulate it. An attempt will be made to find how to make machines use language, form abstractions and concepts, solve kinds of problems now reserved for humans, and improve themselves. We think that a significant advance can be made in one or more of these problems if a carefully selected group of scientists work on it together for a summer.

Ideas in the proposal included the idea of computers learning by 'self improvement'. There are also thoughts on creativity:

> A fairly attractive and yet clearly incomplete conjecture is that the difference between creative thinking and imaginative competent thinking lies in the injection of a some [sic] randomness. The randomness must be guided by intuition to be efficient.

It is interesting to see human imagination is thought to be replicable purely through mere randomness, though somehow guided by intuition.

AI as an idea

So, the term AI is less than a century old. Similarly, the term 'robot' was coined as recently as 1920 by the Czech author Karel Čapek.

Yet the idea of making artificial life is a very old one. For example, in classical Greek mythology, Hephaestus is described as having golden robot servants who assisted him in his work: 'Golden attendants resembling young girls quickly came out to aid their lord. The immortal gods granted them intelligence, speech, strength, and knowledge of handiwork.' True, Hephaestus is a god and the endowment of intelligence on his robots is attributed, as in the quote, to the Gods. Yet Daedalus the clever human craftsman of mythology also made living statues. Talos, a kind of giant robot that was created to protect Crete, appears in the myth of Jason and the Argonauts. Interestingly there seems to be some connection made between the creation of such automata and tyranny (Mayor, 2018). 'AI was a cultural phenomenon before it was a technological one' (Cave and Dihal, 2020, 2).

It appears that the idea that we might create a living thing is a very interesting one to humans, because it is not only in Western mythology that myths of robots/AI appear. The volume edited by Cave, Dihal and Dillon (2020) contains chapters exploring the long history of narratives that contribute to our current cultural understanding of AI. In Cave and Dihal (2023) authors of each chapter parallel the earlier book by exploring the very different ways AI is being imagined in different countries around the world.

Cave and Dihal's (2019) analysis of a large number of texts about AI (primarily from the West, in English) suggest that there are four recurrent dichotomies in how we see AI:

1 The promise of long life or *immortality*, but also a fear of the *loss of humanity* through the changes necessary to gain long life.
2 The promise of *ease* from many burdens, of work, but a fear of being thus made *obsolescent*, of the loss of a role.
3 The lure of *gratification* of our every desire, but risk of *alienation* as we lose contact with other humans.
4 The idea of *domination* of AI but the threat of a robot *uprising*, of out-of-control autonomous systems.

This set of recurrent hopes and fears seems to thread throughout discourses about AI.

AI and Speculative Fiction

AI and robots are central themes in the genre of SF (Science or Speculative Fiction). A lot of our thoughts have been shaped by such works, such as by the three laws of robotics invented by Isaac Azimov. AI is so important to contemporary imagination that more mainstream authors like Ian McKewan and Kazuo Ishiguro have written recent novels about it

Even if we are not SF readers, we are likely to have seen movies and TV series like *Star Wars* or *Star Trek* which include AI/robot characters. There have been several hundred films about AI and robots over the years. Some are positive images, like R2D2 and C-3PO or Data, but often rather dark imaginings as Hal in *2001: A Space Odyssey*, or Skynet from *Terminator*. The TV series *Black Mirror* is a central reference point for speculation about the risks of AI.

As we mentioned in the previous chapter, there is a two-way relationship between such fictions and science, with SF writers often basing their stories on real or predicted science. Movie directors such as Steven Spielberg, work closely with scientists to take their most cutting-edge ideas and try to visualise how they might work in practice. Equally, we know that scientists, including computer scientists, read and even cite SF in their work. Some attempt to build in practice what SF has imagined.

Interestingly, John McCarthy himself also wrote some SF short stories. Perhaps this was an outlet to explore more controversial dimensions. Thus, in his story 'The Robot and the Baby' (McCarthy, 2004) he expresses his doubts about giving household robots any sort of emotions or anything that can have emotion ascribed to it. The story revolves around a robot that breaks existing rules by caring for a baby that has been neglected by its mother. Interestingly, in the story he imagines that a law has been passed preventing robots having emotions or talking to young children. Robots are designed to be fragile on the outside so that when they are kicked something will fall off. In the story the robot breaks the law. Amusingly the confrontation with the authorities is viewed by 7 billion spectators. The robot follows directives in an entirely logical way, challenging the demands from humans. What is most interesting is the deep divisions and controversies the story evokes.

AI in popular culture: metaphors for AI

So, AI is far from the usual technology for which we struggle to make any sense of: it has got a rich cultural resonance.

In a 2025 blog post, Doug Belshaw (2025), offers visualisations of eight contemporary metaphors for AI, as:

- a god
- a spy
- a magician
- a crystal ball
- a black box
- an expert
- a hall of mirrors
- a creative tool.

Each metaphor reflects a different idea or story about what AI is. Yet, each one is rather different, reflecting the multiplicity and rather confusing nature of AI. I notice that many of Belshaw's visualisations shows AI as a human, when of course it is not. Reflecting on the list it immediately occurred to me we could also represent AI as a thief (of our data and content), a secretary (I have heard many students talk about AI in these terms) or a tool to make us more productive (perhaps visualised as a stopwatch).

A *Wired* magazine issue in November 2025 referred to AI as having 'a thousand faces' including:

- teacher
- Americaniser
- therapist
- mother
- start up
- weapon.

Friend or lover is not on the list, but there are a number of stories in the news about young people with growing attachment to AI.

In a piece of research with digital humanists (Ma, Dedema and Cox, 2026) we found AI described through the metaphor of:

- research assistant
- student
- dancing bear (something surprising but basically useless)
- a tool.

The last metaphor is particularly interesting and pervasive. It is often repeated in a way that it is not even recognised as a metaphor, by referring to AI as 'just a tool', implying that its risks only arise from how well or safely it is used. But by that logic, a hand grenade is just a tool. Tools have in-built biases and assumptions. The affordances of AI appropriate and shape us!

Examining these metaphors, the overall impression is that, yes, AI can be all these things, at different moments. It's a multiple and contested idea. Roe, Perkins and Furze (2025) suggest that some metaphors are particularly useful for raising critical AI literacy, such as AI as a funhouse mirror or a black box.

The imagery of AI

Despite the multiplicity of metaphors for AI, if we examine the imagery of AI in the media it is nearly always presented in the form of a robot head or body, overlaid with various numbers or network diagrams (to signify computing and data), usually against a cool blue background (perhaps to imply lack of emotion or masculinity). A search on Google for 'AI' will confirm this pattern. Most blogs or articles or book covers lazily use such imagery. Our visual imagination of AI is very constrained by what we see in such articles.

This imagery bears little relation to what AI really is. It is not very effectively representing that it is about statistics and huge quantities of data. It gestures towards the human and individual and visible. It implies that AI is mistakeable for a human, when most current AI is narrow and merely processes data. On the one hand, it implies the visibility of AI, when it is often actually invisible and infrastructural; at the same time it renders invisible the human actors and organisations that make AI possible across the supply chains of software and hardware.

The wonderful Better Images of AI (2025) offers many alternatives. Let us expand our imagination by presenting a few of these in Figures 2.1–2.4.

Figure 2.1 *AI is everywhere* (Ariyana Ahmad & The Bigger Picture, https://betterimagesofai.org / https://creativecommons.org/licenses/by/4.0)

- *Figure 2.1* 'AI is everywhere' gestures to the pervasive presence of AI in human everyday lives.
- *Figure 2.2* 'Ground up' wonderfully captures the way that AI harvests high and low culture and churns out text like a meat mincer.
- *Figure 2.3* 'Data worker' points to the exploitation of the data worker labelling toxic content.
- *Figure 2.4* 'Who is AI made of?' also visualises the human labour, especially in the majority world, that makes the AI industry possible but is often rendered invisible.

Figure 2.2 *Ground Up and Spat Out by Janet Turra & Cambridge Diversity Fund* (janetturra.wordpress.com/www.race-equality.admin.cam.ac.uk/university-diversity-fund)

Figure 2.3 *Data worker* (Janet Turra, https://betterimagesofai.org, https://creativecommons.org/licenses/by/4.0)

Figure 2.4 *Who is AI made of?* (Shady Sharify, https://betterimagesofai.org, https://creativecommons.org/licenses/by/4.0)

If we were to visualise AI in other ways we might want to capture the sense of AI as automation, through an image of a neat warehouse with robots scooting about picking items for despatch or robots in a car-making factory. In many ways AI is seen through the lens of automation and the mechanisation of tasks.

We might also seek to represent it as something working away in the background infrastructure, shaping our experiences in ways we do not always understand or even realise, as in recommendation and filtering on a streaming platform or social media. Maybe it is something like control mechanisms operating over traffic in a city.

AI technologies

Of course, when we use the term AI today it is primarily to refer to some sort of computing technology. So let us consider some contemporary definitions of the technology of AI.

It is useful to establish the distinction between 'narrow' or 'weak' and 'general' AI. Narrow AI performs a very specific function, such as filtering e-mail for spam. In contrast, general AI is the aspiration for AI to recreate something akin to human intelligence that can adjust to any context. OpenAI's ChatGPT, in the range of things it does, is obviously somewhat nearer to general AI than a spam filter. Indeed, the stated objective of many tech companies is to achieve general AI. Yet if falls far short of a true general AI in being able to perform the range of things a human can perform.

Let us examine some attempts to define what AI technologies are and do.

'AI is the ability of a computer system to solve problems and perform tasks that would otherwise require human intelligence' (US National Security Commission on AI, 2021). This is an example of a very common formulation: that AI is any computer system that performs tasks which are normally expected to require human intelligence. This seems a rather circular definition, because it defines computer intelligence by referring to human intelligence, which is itself not defined. However, of course, it is accurate to say that the focus of AI has always been on the replication of human intelligence. In a way it is odd and disappointing that AI should be imagined solely in terms of simulating human intelligence, with all its limitations, rather than creating another form of intelligence. Perhaps there is also an element of privileging intelligence as if it were the highest function of a human being (echoing the historic discourse privileging IQ). It is also odd that we have the idea of robot to parallel the human body and AI to replicate the mind, when we know body and mind are inseparable for humans, and of course work in tandem with emotions.

'Machines that imitate some features of human intelligence, such as perception, learning, reasoning, problem-solving, language interaction and creative work' (UNESCO, 2022, 9). The UNESCO formulation gives a bit more detail about the kind of tasks that AI performs, but critically also uses the term 'imitate' to rightly reference the fact that while AI does things that humans do, it does it in a different way. Its outputs appear to be intelligent, but that does not imply understanding. It 'learns' or is 'trained' but this process is nothing much like how humans learn. Computers learn by being given huge quantities of data and identifying statistical patterns. In this sense computer intelligence is nothing like how humans make sense or learn about things, though of course how humans think is itself not well understood by science.

'A suite of technologies and tools that aim to reproduce or surpass abilities in computational systems that would require 'intelligence' if humans were to perform them. This could include the ability to learn and adapt; to sense, understand and interact; to reason and plan; to act autonomously; or even create. It enables us to use and make sense of data' (UKRI, 2021, 4). The UKRI (UK Research and Innovation) definition emphasises that AI is an umbrella term for multiple technologies. The scare quotes around the word intelligence point to the difficulties of defining this concept itself. If we are not sure what human intelligence is, saying what computer-based intelligence is will be hard! Like the UNESCO definition, it suggests some tasks AI can perform, here drawing strong parallels between the various functions that define humanity and AI.

'An AI system is a machine-based system that, for explicit or implicit objectives, infers, from the input it receives, how to generate outputs such as predictions, content, recommendations, or decisions that can influence physical or virtual environments. Different AI systems vary in their levels of autonomy and adaptiveness after deployment' (OECD, 2024). The OECD definition is much more complex and it has evolved over time, reflecting changing perceptions of AI, but the need to try and pin down a definition in a regulatory or policy context. Again, we have the list of functions like prediction, content creation, recommendation. 'Inference' is what the system does in relation to its inputs. Usefully, this definition identifies key aspects of the technology, such as its relative autonomy, its ability to act independently of humans, and adaptiveness, its ability to evolve and 'learn'. The positioning of humans in relation to AI is an important aspect here. OECD mention that textbook examples of AI may not be considered to be AI by the public. Indeed, a common observation about AI is that when it becomes familiar it ceases to be labelled as AI. For example, optical character recognition (OCR), the technology to digitise text in libraries and archives, is by most formal definitions AI but is rarely mentioned because it is now considered every day. This implies that AI is always about the future or the future in the present. It is inherently a discourse that is always looking forward and making promises to perform clever things, that now seem nearly impossible. Another example of the way that AI defies being tied down.

'Simply put, AI is a collection of technologies that combine data, algorithms and computing power' (European Commission, 2020, 2). This is a useful definition because it reinforces the sense that current AI is based on data. Earlier rounds of AI attempted to mimic human intelligence in other ways, such as through symbolic logic. But the heart of current AI is machine learning, which is more about algorithms being trained with large amounts of data. Data could be numeric data but could be texts or sound files. Many of the algorithms being deployed today are not new. What is new is that the digitisation of life has made available data on a huge scale that enables AI to perform at a high level. The whole big data discourse in 2000s and 2010s was an essential precursor of AI. The idea was that data was the new 'oil' and a key asset for the insights it offered. Of course, these claims were always contested by those concerned with such issues as privacy, bias in historic data and the inherent limits on what data can tell us. To a large extent those same debates continue around AI.

The EC definition also points to the need for computing power, which is the nearest any of these definitions point to the infrastructure of computing needed to perform AI. What is missing slightly from these definitions is anything about the nature of the algorithms, that they look for statistical patterns and have an inherent element of accuracy or inaccuracy.

Cave, Dihal and Dillon (2020, 4) define AI as 'a heterogeneous network of technologies – including machine learning, natural language processing, expert systems, deep learning, computer vision, and robotics – which have in common the automation of functions of the human brain'. This definition defines AI in terms of types of technologies. It is an umbrella term.

Another useful definition focusing on the multiplicity of AI is the following:

> . . . any software technology with at least one of the following capabilities: perception – including audio, visual, textual, and tactile (e.g. face recognition), decision making (e.g. medical diagnosis systems), prediction (e.g. weather forecasting), automatic knowledge extraction and pattern recognition from data (e.g. discovery of fake news circles in social media), and logical reasoning (e.g. theory development from premises). This new encompasses a large variety of subfields, including machine learning.
>
> (Vinuesa et al., 2020)

This focuses less on the type of function and how it might be applied.

Another term applied to AI is that it is a 'general-purpose' technology. This implies multiple uses in different contexts.

Generative AI, diffusion models, LLMs

While AI is a technology that has been around a rather long time and an idea that seems to be almost as old as humanity, the concept of generative AI is relatively new. Large-language models (LLMs) like Bert were being used in libraries for a while before ChatGPT. But the launch of ChatGPT in November 2022, its rapid rise in use and evolution, have shifted much public attention to the generative AI story.

In simple terms large-language models are text predictors. They have been trained on vast amounts of texts (their 'data') to calculate the probability of how a sentence is likely to be continued. For example, given the start of the sentence 'the cat sat on the . . .' most of us would guess 'mat'. Working on such calculations of probability LLMs are able to predict a reasonable sounding response to our prompts. This does not imply understanding or consciousness, only the ability to calculate patterns in the statistical probabilities of occurrences of words.

Interestingly, when I asked the large-language model Gemini to explain how LLMs work it persisted in using the analogy of a librarian who has read everything and so can predict what else is written.

Image generation is more often performed using GANs (Generative Adversarial Network), where Generators put forwards images and improve it successively from comments from a Discriminator. Interestingly, Gemini suggested to me to use the analogy of a forger gradually improving a forgery. Many in the would agree it's a form of forgery!

At the time of writing, what many imagine AI to be is an AI chatbot, like ChatGPT. This is because it performs a wide range of tasks rapidly and relatively effectively, such as:

- summarising a document
- writing text
- proofreading text
- brainstorming ideas
- writing computer code
- giving advice
- creating images
- drafting plans.

This makes ChatGPT and the, like a multipurpose service that can help in many contexts. For example, if someone is writing a report they might use it to:

- analyse data
- generate a structure for a report
- draft sections
- manage the time of the author.

It is a more general form of AI than most we have encountered before, because it takes on this wide range of tasks. Presenting AI as a chatbot is a clever device to generate human trust. AI chatbots tend to be given a chatty, positive, helpful persona. This can be seen as clever design, but it is also misleading, because of course the AI is not in any way human. It also implicitly exaggerates the capabilities of AI (van Es and Nguyen, 2025). The same can be said of the way that ChatGPT refers to itself as a person in conversation with users, when it is not. It seems that people begin to forget that it is not human. Fundamentally it is AI designed to generate satisfied customers rather than a critical thinker or engaged citizen. This is far from inherent to the technology. So, a particular narrative is embedded in the technology.

For many people, at the time of writing, free AI chatbots or image generators represent what AI is. This reflects the power of Big Tech companies with their vast resources of money, computing power and data to control the direction of technology development and the meaning of the idea of AI. Although AI is an idea, it's one with huge value according to stock market valuations of AI companies. But it is important to remember that this is only one type of AI, implemented in a very particular type of way.

Often when AI is represented by Big Tech it is linked to some recurrent storylines of technology, such as that it is a prime mover of change and a solution to social ills. Indeed, we can say that the AI hype reproduces three persistent myths that so often appear in discourses around technology, even though they have been widely questioned by scholars.

Firstly, there is the myth that the development and use of technology is autonomous. Rather than humans inventing or making AI for societal good or organisations developing and adopting it for competitive benefit, the technology seems to be the driver of change in itself. It evolves on its own path and society merely reacts and follows.

Secondly, the change coming with technology is presented as inevitable: change will come regardless of what humans do. We have no choice. This assumption is called 'technological determinism'. These claims have material effects: the belief that we have no choice but to adopt AI underscores, inevitably, compulsion to learn how to use it. Fear of missing out. Actually, we know that if commercial interests shift, technologies can stop being developed. Voice assistants like Siri provide one relevant example, where they seemed to 'be the future', but seem to have stalled in their development because focus has shifted to other technologies.

The third myth is that technologies can in themselves solve complex social challenges like climate change or global poverty. Such 'technological solutionism' is again a pervasive story around technologies. We can see this in news stories about AI-based medical interventions curing a disease. Such solutions are dependent on human uses of the technology. And when we think about the complex social problems they require multiple actions at many different levels.

So, a dominant narrative around technology, repeated within discourses about AI, is that it is an autonomous driver of inevitable change that can solve humanity's problems. These myths are repeated so often that they are hard to think beyond (Markham, 2021).

Fortunately, AI is more challenged than most technologies. The ethical and societal impacts of AI always seem to emerge in the story. The next chapter considers some of these, but it is noticeable that nearly every story around AI has to grapple with the many doubts we have about it.

What AI is

For practical purposes we might best see AI as a technology which given the right data and a well-chosen algorithm may helpfully perform a range of tasks:

- inputting – turning speech, images, text or handwritten text into computer-readable data, e.g. interpreting a spoken query;
- transcribing – e.g. producing a searchable transcript of a video, enabling in depth search;
- outputting – producing results in the form of text, voice, images, video, e.g. producing outputs from a search in an audible form;
- classifying – identifying clusters of similar items in data, e.g. identifying the type of a plant from a photograph;
- summarising – producing an abstract or lay summary;
- filtering – e.g. sorting e-mail into spam, important and regular messages;
- recommending – matching content to a user based on classifying content and matching it to users based on their past behaviour (like browsing habits) or an individual or group profile, e.g. suggesting books of interest;

- translating – e.g. taking a book in and translating it for a non-native English speaker;
- predicting – analysing past data to predict future patterns, e.g. estimating how many people might come to the library on a rainy day in November;
- Generating – creating text or images based on a prompt, e.g. producing a draft of text following the style of a policy document.

A few years ago, as in the Vinuesa et al. (2020) definition above, we would not have included generation. The AI promise changes all the time. 2025 was predicted to be the year of agentic AI (Paul, 2024). That may not have fully materialised: future predictions often compress the time period over which change happens. But agentic AI does appear to be the likely next manifestation of AI. The concept of agentic AI is used to make many promises (Cox, 2025b). But central is the idea that AI is able to perform a series of tasks with a degree of independence in making decisions. AIIM (Association of Intelligent Information Management) define it thus: 'AI agents are autonomous digital entities that use intelligence to automate tasks often involving multiple steps and decisions. These agents are capable of addressing complex objectives, processing information, responding intelligently to inputs and improving over time' (AIIM, 2025).

We have seen some automation of complex processes through technologies like Robotic Process Automation. This is similar, but with a greater ability to make decisions:

> AI agency is a spectrum. At one end, traditional systems with limited agency perform specific tasks under narrowly defined conditions. At the other end, future agentic AI systems with full agency will learn from their environment, make decisions and perform tasks independently. . . . Agentic AI refers to goal-driven software entities that have been granted rights by the organization to act on its behalf autonomously, make decisions and take action.
>
> (Coshow et al., 2024)

In a way the agentic AI idea is relatively simple: it's the way that a series of tasks are chained together, then carried out, with necessary decisions being made by the AI along the way.

Agentic AI is often pictured interacting with humans or even with other agents. In many ways this is just one further step towards the strong AI vision that inspires many developments.

AI is a rapidly evolving concept, though it would be fair also to point to the many limits of current AI which include fundamental points:

- A lack of true understanding and certainly no feelings or ethical commitments
- No grasp of context
- No consciousness or personhood

The politics and political economy of AI

The commercial investment in myths of AI made by Big Tech is matched by the statements of governments all around the world keen to find ways to latch onto the magic of AI to solve societal problems. It often seems that they also reproduce the three myths about technology. It reflects the hope that AI can deal with hard-to-solve problems like the claimed inefficiencies of government administration or the health problems of an aging population making huge demands on health services or the claim that workforces have low productivity.

An important alternative perspective is offered by critical scholars such as Crawford (2021). Here AI is an industry. It has tentacles all across the globe. AI is not just about answering our question or saving time on making notes on meetings. It is as much about harsh conditions for miners digging for copper or the traumatic experiences of those having to view inappropriate content to exclude it from the training data for an LLM and the suffering caused to communities by polluting resource extraction or e-waste, or water shortages caused by a new data centre. It is an industry driven by an aspiration to make money. These experiences should be as part of our imagination of AI as ChatGPT's garrulous answers to our prompts. Estampa (2024) map out the many exploitative relationships that lie behind generative AI. Much of the talk about AI fuels, and is fuelled by, stock market prices. The hype around AI has its origin in large part in the financial rewards at stake (Thais, 2024). The dent made in Nvidia shares by the launch of the Chinese LLM Deepseek revealed the critical commercial interests at stake. The recurrent stories in 2025 about an AI bubble reinforce the sense of the economic drivers.

AI is also a focus of geo-political struggle, with USA and China warring for dominance.

This is not necessarily the case; the idea of public or community AI suggests alternative models where AI is like other public utility infrastructure such as roads, developed for the public good, with an emphasis on equitable access and accountability (Sieker et al., 2025).

Certainly, we have to recognise that AI is a strategic concern. For example, in the UK there have been multiple government AI strategies (and separate ones for devolved nations such as Scotland). There is an AI strategy for the UK's National Health Service and the main research funders (UKRI). There are national-level educational strategies, as well as those within individual HE institutions.

When we are using an AI chatbot these realities may be far from our mind, but they should not be, because ultimately the business strategies of AI companies is impacting lives of people all around the globe.

Competing stories of AI

Looking beyond specific technologies and applications, AI seems to be linked to a number of promises and attendant risks – see Table 2.1 – that we often hear repeated. We do not always notice that different promises are being made in different contexts. It is hard not to represent these through a series of dualisms, though that may not be helpful.

Table 2.1 *Competing visions of the benefits and risks of AI*

Benefit of AI	Risk of AI
Increased access to knowledge, e.g. through translation, summarisation and/or improved and easier search	A crisis of information through a stream of AI 'slop' and deepfakes undermining trust in all information, and accelerating plausible deniability of any statement
Greater efficiencies, e.g. automating data processing and increased productivity, e.g. making it quicker to write a report from data	Displacement of work by automation of certain tasks that may be deemed to be routine or mundane (even if people enjoy doing them or depend on them for their livelihoods) plus acceleration of pressures on people to produce more quickly. More self-service enabled by AI rather than real empowerment
Richer, individualised learning, e.g. through adaptivity of content to our stage of learning and the different ways we learn	A loss of critical thinking as essential thinking and learning tasks are offloaded onto AI
Enhanced creativity, e.g. supporting ideation for documents or activities	An echo chamber for original ideas appropriated without consent or attribution, crowding out our own originality
Deeper intelligence and closer control, e.g. through analysing and predicting from data including human behaviour and supplying better management information to managers	Greater surveillance and control, loss of privacy, greater security threats and a loss of human autonomy

A final thought is that AI may be part of a wider set of technologies that collectively are changing how society and organisations work over the longer term, including social media and virtual and augmented reality. Often the digital transformation or fourth industrial revolution agenda refers to a wide range of technologies that together change how organisations can work. Even though AI is itself multiple, it could also be seen as part of a wider cluster of technologies that collectively shift how things are done. The digital transformation discourse is another idea associated with AI.

Conclusion

In this chapter we have revealed the many ways AI is talked about, as a branch of computer science invented at a particular time and place, a pervasive subject of myth and storytelling, a global industry.

What does seem to be clear is that AI is essentially an idea and as such indeterminate (open to change and redefinition) and multiple. It is these qualities that our narrative approach to AI seeks to benefit from, prompting imaginative engagement and a sense of our own agency in inventing what AI means, albeit there are powerful commercial and political interests also trying to control it.

We are used to technology changing and having to adjust. So, what can we learn from past experience? This depends on what analogy we chose. Is the arrival of generative AI:

- like the calculator which was seen as a threat to basic skills in arithmetic, but is now taken for granted?
- like Wikipedia, thought at first to be a dangerously uncontrolled form of knowledge, now accepted as a valid source?
- like the arrival of Google Search and Amazon recommendation, that at first were seen as threats to information discovery but changed how search worked?
- like spell-checking in word processors, potentially undercutting our ability to write well without help, but now taken for granted?
- like the invention of the internet or the web?
- the 'new electricity' powering a Fourth Industrial Revolution?
- like the power loom with many workers as the handloom weavers made destitute by the mechanisation of their craft?

Activities

The activities for this chapter emphasise thinking about the complex cultural associations of AI.

- What metaphors for AI did you hear today?
- Which metaphor for AI presented above strikes you as having the greatest depth and power?

- How would you visualise AI? In their paper on imaginaries of data, Benabdallah, Kaneko and Desjardins (2023), recognising the difficulty that the public have in understanding the concept of data, prompted participants to imagine data in different ways. They used the following questions. They then tried to intervene to shift these imaginaries. Consider these same questions for AI:
  - What materials do you associate with it?
  - What might data sound like?
  - What might data feel like?
  - What might data smell like?
  - How might data move?
  - Where do data go?
  - What adventures might data be part of?
  - What fiction genre do you associate data with?
  - What friends does data make?
  - What characters do you associate with data?
- Try visualising AI using your favourite image generator like Stable Diffusion or Craiyon. How does AI represent itself?
- Look at the Better Images of AI (2025) website and pick your favourite representation.

In this story I tried to relate my own privileged experiences of AI with its wider consequences (Cox, 2020). I am not sure how successful it was. What story would you write to explore such issues?

Minnie, the AI admin assistant

I can ask the AI speaker in my office anything about administrative aspects of my job, such as the regulations for the programme I am teaching, the dates by which I need to submit changes to assessment, how many students are predicted to take my module next semester, their predicted grades, and the projected level of plagiarism, even a numerical rating of the alignment between my proposed learning outcomes and the university graduate attributes. It's always very precise.

It alerts me to who is dropping behind in the class.

It warns me when marks are released and reports on student reactions so I can ensure their well-being.

Sometimes I feel it's amazingly insightful. It comes up with suggested actions. It's even giving me foresight on students who are taking my module next semester, from their current performance.

At other times it seems clumsy. It's hard to put one's finger on what makes living with it uncomfortable. I suppose it's quite demanding at times. As a small cog in its machine, I try and smooth out the wrinkles.

I sometimes ponder the global infrastructures that lie behind this small yet miraculous black plastic box:

- All the data mined from my past questions and those of other staff at the university, data on students from this year and the previous ten years, and data bought about staff and students at other universities deemed comparable. All feeding into algorithms owned by an American corporation (not a household name). The board of directors summoned to a late-night meeting to discuss adjusting risk assessments in response to inside intelligence of planned changes in government policy in Brazil.
- A vast effort of digitalisation, partly accomplished by crowdsourcing, paying click-workers fractions of dollars to perform small tasks to hone the algorithm. A young woman in a suburb of Delhi squints at her screen and tries to get a better connection.
- The server farms that host data and content and process it. Corridors of chilly rooms where wires cross and LEDs flicker 24 hours a day.
- Power stations needed to power the networks. A column of steam climbs from a tall chimney hundreds of feet into the clear blue sky.
- The vast effort of global logistics to bring together countless components to build the devices through which we interact with AI. Lorries queuing at the container port as another ship comes in to dock.
- Workers making computer components in hi-tech factories in East Asia. All dressed in the same blue overalls and facemasks, two hundred workers queue patiently waiting to be scan searched as they leave work at the end of the shift.
- Exploitative mining extracting non-renewable, scarce minerals for computer components, polluting the environment and (it is suspected) reducing the life expectancy of local people. Pipes churn out a clayey sludge into a vast lake.

3

AI and Information

This chapter reflects on how generative AI is changing how people search for and use information, specifically from the perspective of the ethical commitments and theories of library and information science (LIS).

The LIS profession

To frame our reflection on the impact of AI this chapter starts by considering the commitments of LIS as a practice and as a discipline.

The core driving principle of LIS practice is to enable free and equitable access to knowledge as a fundamental human right and social good. In different sectors of LIS activity this is manifested differently. Examples are open access to content in the academic domain; the fostering of knowledge sharing within organisations; and the long-term preservation of the cultural record in archives and special collections. The collection, organisation and making accessible of bodies of rich, accurate and reliable information is a central task for LIS, including a commitment to a lack of bias. It implies resistance to censorship and promotion of freedom of expression. It also entails accessibility of information access systems that are transparent for the user, combined with fostering critical information literacy skills for evaluating information so it can be gathered and used appropriately. The task of teaching the critical evaluation of digital information sources in today's highly complex information world is indeed central to a profession increasingly focused on education and training users. It is recognised that such information can come in many forms, especially digital forms, despite the public's over-identification of libraries with books.

LIS is a service-oriented profession, with a strong 'user' focus. While the notion of 'user' has been criticised for implying passivity and failing to acknowledge the diversity among groups, its use in the profession articulates a focus on benefit to people seeking and using information, beyond treating them as customers. Actually, making information available in diverse forms to recognise the diversity among users, such as through accessibility, is a central interest.

At the heart of collecting and giving access to rich, unbiased knowledge is a growing recognition of the value of different knowledge systems and diverse knowledge creators. There is increasing acknowledgement of the need to decentre western, white, male, elite, heterosexual, ableist authored knowledge, which has historically dominated in science and many academic disciplines, and all areas of social knowledge. By extension such biases have predominated in the collections of many libraries. Indeed, one could go further in acknowledging that libraries as institutions have often been closely implicated in problems such as colonialist thinking and are in danger of continuing to do so. We should not see these harms as purely historical: these are ongoing, and some communities feel alienated from libraries like other institutions as a consequence. To overcome these barriers, there is a need for collection thinking to shift as well as a fundamental investment in changing ways of describing collections, and also in staffing of libraries.

While access to knowledge is the principal driver of LIS, it is not wholly unqualified, and there is recognition of the need to respect the privacy of individuals; the confidentiality of organisations; author rights to some reward for their creativity (but also asserting copyright exceptions for libraries); and indigenous ways of governing knowledge which may not align to openness.

The academic discipline of LIS

Aligned to these ethical principles, LIS as an academic discipline is concerned with theories and empirical evidence on how people search for and use information, generally referred to as information behaviour or information practices. Implicit are the same commitments to the importance of access to information and the value of increasing access to knowledge. Whereas the profession seeks to do this in the context of delivering particular services such as in libraries to a user base, LIS as a discipline deals with the study of how people actually search for and use information, across many sources, in different contexts, but the ultimate purpose is the same: to build on this to think about how society's access to knowledge is ensured.

For a long time, search was the key focus, in the context of it being hard to locate reliable information, especially in scientific or corporate decision making. The field of information retrieval deals with the design of search systems that enable people to search effectively. Over time, however, scholarly attention has widened in a number of ways (as summarised in Table 3.1 opposite).

Seeking for information was seen as driven by user information need, often in a decision-making process. People will tend to want high-quality information in this context: that is, accurate, up to date and comprehensive. Part of this implies transparency of retrieval systems, since we need to

Table 3.1 *Shifts in focus in information behaviour research*

Traditional focus	New areas of focus
Intentional, need-driven information search	Information encountering
Search for printed text or information from people	Digital information via computers and smartphones, increasingly mediated by platforms
Search as a purely rational, cognitive process	Embodied and emotional dimensions of information behaviour
Search for scientific or business decision-making purposes	Everyday information seeking and use
Information search	Information use and storage
Context of scarcity	Context of abundance or overload

understand the nature of a source to judge if it is accurate. Seeking information to satisfy a need is a process of stages but often it is iterative and non-linear. Research on information behaviour has found that while often seeking information is intentional and driven by need, it can also be unintentional, through information encountering, browsing or 'foraging', which is less goal-directed. The way that we serendipitously find information has been widely studied.

Although complete and reliable information might be ideal for decision making, in practice people often show satisficing behaviour, where they stop searching even when there is more to discover. The principle of people wanting to save time and effort in information search is a common factor shaping information behaviour.

While the term information seeking implies a primarily cognitive task, another shift is that there is increasing recognition that it has corporeal and emotional dimensions. Information from our bodies in the form of sensory information is important. The body can be used to consciously show information and unconsciously gives off information. Information activities are also emotional processes, with a broad movement from negative feelings of confusion and discomfort tending to be replaced by positive emotions such as confidence as information is uncovered.

In some contexts, people might avoid, actively block or resist information. Information horizons refer to the range of sources that people use to discover information. Often for those in society with the fewest resources the information horizons can also be quite restricted.

Generally, early research examined the scientific or corporate context, particularly relating to finding formally recorded information, although it has always been recognised that other people were an important source of information. One important shift has been away from research or corporate contexts, to include everyday information seeking, in the context of people searching for information for their health, as citizens or for pastimes. It is recognised that within different areas of practice there are very different patterns of use and evaluation of information.

There has also been a shift to reflect more on information use. Hektor's (2001) model of everyday information online is a good starting point for thinking about information use, breaking down the whole information discovery and use process into:

1. search and retrieve – the traditional goal-oriented search
2. browse – a more browsing approach to finding information
3. monitor – watching a site that has updates
4. read and view (Hektor calls this unfolding) – actively watching or reading information sources
5. exchange – giving information to others and receiving it
6. organise – (Hektor calls this dressing)
7. instruct – teach someone else
8. publish – make it public.

Some of the terminology Hektor uses is a little strange, so we have picked better words above, but his model extends our appreciation of what people do with information, not just online. It could be extended further, because it lacks full recognition of the activities of storing, retrieving and displaying information that has been explored in the field called personal information management (PIM). We might slot this under what Hektor calls 'dressing' and we will call 'organise'. The PIM literature shows that people are often information collectors, but these collections tend to be rather disorganised because of factors such as lack of priority, lack of training in organising information, platform change, hybridity and diversity of collections (e.g. it is in different formats, both print and digital, so can't be easily put in one place) (Jones, 2010).

Whereas in the past access to information, generally in printed form, was hard, and there were limited finding aids, now digital, web information, with ubiquitous smartphone access, has created a sense of abundance often of overload of information, rather than information scarcity. From the perspective of the core principle of LIS to give access to knowledge this is welcomed because it is vastly easier than ever before to find information. Social media enables people to themselves create or curate information in new ways. These changes shift the logic of information seeking. It is easier to find a 'good enough' answer to many topics. The domination of certain platforms in information discovery means that understanding how these work to shape information use also becomes a central topic.

The information crisis

At the same time as the availability of information has become so much greater in the last decades, there is a sense of crisis around the quality of information and how it is used, arising from a number of interwoven issues. AI has participated in creating (but also potentially solving) some of these problems:

1. Lack of quality control and the ability of social media to distribute information rapidly, leading to more misinformation (inaccurate information) in circulation. This is linked to the information overload problem, where the competition for attention leads to overwhelming floods of messages and shorter attention spans. AI has both helped to create this flood (e.g. through robots on social media platforms) and to address it through filtering and automated moderation.
2. Commercially driven personalisation and recommendation (based on AI) driven by the need to control the abundance of information but tending to risk creating filter bubbles, where people only receive information reinforcing their assumptions, driving polarisation, and to lead to addiction and digital dependence. Platforms tend to further exclude the perspectives of the marginalised, because they place emphasis on serving users who are seen to have the market power and so be worth influencing.
3. Increasing levels of corporate surveillance and platform control linked to harvesting of data, driven by the desire to have data for its commercial value, including to support AI.
4. Critical inequities of access in society, such as for certain populations with poor internet access or outdated or limited digital and related skills, leading to less ability to access and evaluate information effectively. This has the potential to reinforce social inequality and digital exclusion. Families with less digital access are losing out in multiple ways: through earning less, paying more for goods, and lacking access into the wider cultural life of society.
5. International inequities, meaning that people in some countries, particularly those in the Global South, have less access to information.
6. Predominance of English-language media control/Western media and the domination of the scientific paradigm by Western science and its assumptions.
7. Malevolent actors using platforms like social media to propagate

disinformation (deliberate falsehoods). AI-created deepfakes are part of the problem: AI reinforces the difficulty of identifying what is a real image, though AI can also help spot fakes.
8 Greater vulnerability of individuals and organisations to cyberattack, because of increasing dependence on and value placed on data. Criminals can use AI techniques; equally cyber-security professionals can use AI to protect security. But the datafication of everything is the underlying issue.
9 State censorship, surveillance and propaganda – a long-standing issue in certain contexts, but given new mechanisms through AI.
10 Poor practices of critical evaluation (and secure management) of information among the public, reinforced by information overload and increasingly invisible infrastructural impacts of AI, making it harder to discern disinformation or misinformation.
11 Through many of these processes, there may be a pattern of decaying trust in information generally. This has its positive side in people being more sceptical about what they are told but is also problematic in eroding trust in general and creating plausible deniability.

So, while access to information seems to have greatly increased in most contexts, significant information problems remain, and these often appear to be linked to AI. It is into this context that generative AI arrives on the scene.

The proliferation of generative AI

The launch of a public version of ChatGPT in November 2022 was a critical trigger for the mass take-up of generative AI. The number of AI chatbots quickly proliferated, with Google's Gemini, Claude, Perplexity, and later a Chinese-based LLM, Deepseek.

The functionality of such AI chatbots has itself rapidly evolved, as captured in Table 3.2 opposite.

But as well as the very rapid growth in the number of ChatGPT users, the use of the generative AI functionality has rapidly proliferated across many platforms. A very significant example is the way that Google overviews have been embedded in everyday search. A proportion of all searches now produce an AI summary. We do not know the exact frequency and it is likely to change over time, but the evidence suggests that this changes how people search, with more reliance on the summary than consulting the underlying sources.

Table 3.2 *The evolution of generative AI, focusing on ChatGPT* (Sources: https://techcrunch.com/2025/12/22/chatgpt-everything-to-know-about-the-ai-chatbot; www.searchenginejournal.com/history-of-chatgpt-timeline/488370).

2018 GPT1
2019 GPT2
2020 GPT3
Nov 30 2022 – Release of ChatGPT to public
Feb 1 2023 – ChatGPT Plus launched
Feb 7 2023 – MS Bing starts using ChatGPT
Feb 2023 – ChatGPT Plus released – subscription model
Mar 1 2023 – ChatGPT API
Mar 14 2023 – Anthropic launches Claude
Mar 14 2023 – ChatGPT starts use of GP4
Mar 21 2023 – Google launches Bard
Mar 22 2023 – Open letter suggesting pause on AI
Apr 25 2023 – ChatGPT adds privacy guardrails
May 2023 – ChatGPT Plus web browsing
Aug 2023 – Custom instructions
Sep 2023 – Voice capabilities added to ChatGPT
Nov 2023 – AI Collins Dictionary word of the year
Jan 2024 – GPTstore launched
Feb 2024 – Bard renamed Gemini
May 2024 – GPT-4o 'Omni' – multimodal AI launch
May 2024 – Google AI overviews released in USA
Aug 2024 – 200 million weekly users claimed
Jan 2025 – Deepseek launched
Mar 2025 – ChatGPT adopts MCP (Model Context Protocol)
Jul 2025 – ChatGPT Study mode launched
Aug 2025 – GPT-5
Sep 2025 – 700 million weekly users claimed
Oct 2025 – Launch of ChatGPT browser, Atlas
Dec 2025 – ChatGPT voice and tone can now be adjusted

We see generative AI also in institutionally configured local tools like Microsoft Copilot and web services aimed at particular communities such as researchers, like Scite, Consensus and SciSpace. Gradually databases that libraries subscribe to such as Scopus, Web of Science and library management systems increasingly have generative AI embedded in them.

Indeed, in their effort to compete with the AI chatbots, many specialist tools have introduced generative AI functionality. A significant example is the incorporation of an AI that summarises a text. Tools such as Adobe Acrobat Reader now actively offer AI summaries. This means that it is hard to avoid generative AI functionality, even if one does not fully realise its nature at the point of use. However, because these often draw on Big Tech technologies in difficult-to-discern ways, they may reproduce some of their problems.

We only have fragmentary information about how these changes are impacting human information behaviour. A 2025 study showed that a quarter of all requests to ChatGPT were for information (Chatterji et al., 2025). But information requests were defined quite narrowly to mean specific information requests, and searches for purchases or recipes. Under some of the other categories, such as 'seeking guidance', there was probably also what LIS would consider information seeking. Activities related to information use such as writing were also important.

This is a high-level summary of use. As a whole we lack research on the big picture of how AI is changing information behaviour, but we can guess it is having a significant effect. One precious piece of evidence is a YouGov study in the UK in early 2025 which revealed the level of trust in AI chatbots for different kinds of questions (Smith, 2025). The British public thought AI chatbots were very good or fairly good at the following:

- 65% answering general knowledge enquires
- 63% proof-reading writing
- 54% drafting e-mails
- 50% providing summaries of complex topics
- 39% writing essays on academic topics
- 35% coming up with good creative writing
- 27% solving business problems
- 21% legal advice
- 17% diagnosing a medical issue
- 12% providing good relationship advice.

The data is limited to the UK, and relatively old, coming from the beginning of 2025, but it is suggestive. There does seem a sense that AI chatbots have quickly gained quite a high level of trust for a wide range of tasks, including information seeking.

A study later in the year (Ofcom, 2025) suggests that UK users like to use AI Chatbots for "low stakes" questions, but are much more wary when researching important issues like finance or health. For these questions they continue to prefer Google search.

Another part of the YouGov study reveals that usage is very divided by age. Thus 53% of 18–24-year-olds were using it at least once a week, whereas those above 65 years old this was more like 2%. There is thus an extremely strong division by age, at least in this study.

There have been many studies of student use of generative AI. For example, a study of UK undergraduates found a rapid shift from 47% of them not using AI in their assessment at all in early 2024 to just 12% in early 2025 (Freeman, 2025). They were using it for:

- explaining concepts (58%)
- summarising articles (48%)
- suggesting research ideas (41%)
- structuring thoughts (39%)
- using AI suggested text after editing (25%).

On a slightly more positive note, many held concerns about using AI, such as:

- getting false results (53%)
- getting biased results (37%)
- privacy (22%)
- loss of learning opportunities (18%)
- training of AI on content without authorial consent (14%)
- environmental impact (13%).

Thus, there is awareness of some of the issues around AI.

Information benefits of AI chatbots

Search, as prototypically represented by Google for many years, involves entering some keywords into a search box and getting back a list of resources, ranked by relevance. There are many problems with this, such as how ranking is determined partly by commercial motives and the user's limited persistence and criticality in examining results. Library discovery systems have mimicked many aspects of Google search, because it is arguably more accessible than advanced Boolean search through careful vocabularies. They have sought to recreate the same one search space for everything that Google offers. It seems that AI chatbots may be resetting search expectations.

Generative AI can be seen as a new paradigm of search, for three aspects of what it offers. Firstly, we can pose our question in natural language, rather than trying to pick exactly the right terms that encapsulate our question. Indeed, generative AI copes better with misspelling and our poor articulations of our questions because from the context of a whole expression it can detect intent.

Secondly, generative AI offers an iterative conversation, rather than a one-off search query, so there is an opportunity to make it clear what the query is (indeed to understand it better oneself) through a form of dialogue. Careful wording of prompts can optimise results, but AI chatbots work fairly well to develop a useful answer through conversation.

Thirdly, and above all, AI chatbots give an answer to a question, rather than a list of resources that we then have to make the effort to locate and read.

As such they offer a very 'user friendly' way of accessing information – easier than Google search or a library search. In those many cases when we are seeking a good enough answer to a question a chatbot gives us one, rather than a list of references we have to consult. It can also summarise or synthesise a debate. Given the desire of people in their information behaviour to save time and effort and the genuine difficulty of synthesising an answer from many sources, these abilities are appealing.

As such, AI chatbots can be seen as helping to meet what we have seen is one of the prime drivers of LIS – increasing access to information and knowledge. As we shall see in the next sections, there are many qualifications of the quality of the information given, but ease of access to information partly explains the popularity of AI chatbots.

AI chatbots are also conversational and friendly. This can perhaps also be seen to mimic a quality of a favourite information source – other people – at the same time as offering responses 24/7 at will, in a way human information givers do not. Indeed, searching for information has always been recognised to be an emotional journey, with considerable discomfort and uncertainty particularly at the beginning of the process. AI chatbots are positive and helpful in a way that users are likely to find addresses the emotional as well as informational aspects of searching.

AI chatbots have some other strengths: they not only offer question answering, but have a wide range of other functions that support the use of information (e.g. in writing, brainstorming ideas, structuring a writing plan, paraphrasing and rewording, proof-reading, creating images to represent data or ideas). This broad set of information-use functions means they are a single place of support to information tasks, unlike a library catalogue, which only supports one part of the activity – or even Google.

In addition to informational uses AI chatbots offer many other services, such as time management advice, advice on drafting communications and so forth. There is evidence of increasing use for companionship and support. The reliability of such support may be questionable, but it is valued by some. AI also offers increased access to knowledge through translation of different languages. This is perhaps the most exciting development in widening access to knowledge. AI also increases accessibility of information in terms of transforming information, e.g. presenting information in a form suitable for different ages or levels of understanding. AI might be good at creating lay summaries of health information, though there must be concerns about accuracy.

Added together these abilities mean that accessing and using information is easier and, in many ways, richer with AI chatbots. For these reasons some have predicted that generative AI marks the end of search as we have known it (Amer and Elboghdadly, 2024). However, information professionals feel a deep dilemma here, because there are a whole range of ways in which AI chatbots, as realised by Big Tech, fall terribly short of sound information inquiry systems, as LIS principles would hope for. These faults are not all inherent in the technology of LLMs: often they are to do with how they have been developed so far by Big Tech. The AI chatbots are the examples most in use. As skilled information searchers, information professionals recoil from simply making things easier, without the concern for quality. The dilemma is about how far and in what way can its use be recommended.

Information problems of AI chatbots

The following sections outline the issues with AI chatbots from an information-behaviour perspective. Some are inherent to the technology (LLMs), some arise from decisions made by Big Tech in realising the technology in the form of AI chatbots.

Accuracy

A major problem is the accuracy of answers and the nature of trust in AI chatbots as information sources.

LLMs predict text based on the data they are trained on. They are not, as is often hoped for, an organisational chatbot, based on 'a single point of truth' where preliminary work is conducted to identify reliable answers that the chatbot can respond with. AI chatbots have been trained on a large range of content, but these contain many inaccuracies. Data can be outdated. The web is reported to be an important source for training AI chatbots. But as we know, not everything on the web is accurate, and it is certainly not a full representation of expressions of human knowledge. There is no stage in constructing an answer by an AI chatbot of a check for accuracy. Indeed, most AI chatbots do state at the bottom of each response web page that answers can be inaccurate and advise users to check.

> ChatGPT can make mistakes. Check important info.
> Gemini can make mistakes, including about people, so double-check it.

A level of inaccuracy is true of any source, but users rarely fully understand the nature of answers from an AI chatbot, so it makes it hard to fully take this into account. We know a single-authored work might have certain types of issues of reliability. We know how to read from a newspaper article based on how it might be biased because of its political stance. We are in new territory with AI chatbots. We have quoted evidence that UK students are aware of some of the problems, but there is still a significant minority of them not even acknowledging the problem.

AI use for slop, misinformation and disinformation

We already saw how information overload has been seen as a long-term problem, necessitating the creation of filtering and moderation, which themselves can use AI but also create their own problems. It is a problem in everyday life, where we are bombarded with information demanding our attention. It is also a problem in academia, where the amount being published has vastly accelerated. Generative AI seems to further worsen this problem by generating loads of low-quality content (slop) and making it easier to create and distribute misinformation and disinformation (Read, 2024). Indeed, a study has suggested that by November 2024 there are more articles being produced on the internet purely by AI than by humans (Paredes et al., 2024). The evidence also supports the idea that humans are fairly bad at detecting AI-created text and images, yet they may overestimate their ability to do so (e.g. Köbis, Doležalová and Soraperra, 2021).

The benefits of AI answers and Google overviews often are seen to address issues of overload, by providing synthesis, but how trustworthy these are and the impacts on understanding need to be considered.

Bias and cultural imbalance

It can be obvious that an answer is wrong, but bias in answers is perhaps a more insidious issue. Bias and cultural imbalance are fundamental issues with

AI chatbots (Hu et al., 2025). Given that they were trained largely on open web content, where English-language material from the Global North predominates, they are always going to be likely to be culturally biased. Certain sources that seem to have been privileged are not representative. For example, the high use of Reddit for training AI is a concern, because it is populated mostly by US youth. Attempts to curate training data through labelling can again introduce bias. The data used to train AI is far from neutral. Importantly, as Kerche, Zook and Graham (2026) argue, patterns in availability of training data and the hidden assumptions in that data are not just an unfortunate mischance but represent the workings of patterns of historic and continuing power and privilege. Big Tech's AI reproduces the cultural assumptions of the West.

If historic data is biased, training AI on that data will reproduce the bias. A classic example was when Amazon used biased historic data to train a recruitment tool, resulting in perpetuation of their hiring bias (Rafi, 2024). There is long-standing evidence that Google search results were biased. The obvious examples being that if you search for 'doctor' you tend to get pictures of white men; if you search for 'nurse' you get images of women. It is biased in the sense that it does not represent the range and diversity of these professions; also biased in that while there may be some basis to these representations, it is not helpful to reinforce stereotypes. Bias can be covert (Hofmann et al., 2024). Representing things in biased ways actively excludes minoritised groups when they see their own experiences misrepresented. For some, the lack of nuance in AI reduces everything to stereotypes (Turk, 2023). This arises from lack of depth of data beyond Western perspectives.

Kerche, Zook and Graham (2026) suggest that AI has a 'trope bias' which leads it to repeat easy stereotypes and an 'averaging bias' that means it tends to give easy summaries, rather than acknowledge complexity.

Another kind of bias is the way that guardrails are put in place to stop AI chatbots responding about certain types of potentially controversial topics. This is effectively a form of censorship, blocking inquiries about a legitimate topic. The way that AI chatbots tend to agree with you heightens the risk of confirmation bias: it is not going to challenge you to rethink your assumptions.

One could certainly argue that given the human tendency to have all sorts of conscious and unconscious bias, AI might have the potential to be less biased, since we can curate data inputs and configure it. The reality of AI chatbots developed by Big Tech is not a low level of bias, rather it amplifies them.

Information sources are unclear

At a fundamental level AI chatbots often fail to give a clear sense of where their answers are derived from. Sources are sparsely cited, if at all. This makes it harder to check answers for accuracy, even if the chatbot itself includes a statement recommending that important information needs to be checked. It also models a less than desirable practice of sharing information without giving evidence or a source. Indeed, it is well known to information professionals that AI chatbots invent citations. Often genuine authors and real journals are cited but the references given in AI chatbots do not actually exist. Furthermore, AI chatbots tend to give a different answer to a question each time, so their own answers cannot be referenced easily.

Collectively these features undercut the whole regime of knowledge construction, where the sources for an idea are given, so that the reader can check them should they wish to do so. Checking is different from finding out in a holistic way, and might involve certain types of approach and skills we are not trained in. It is true that this is not always explicitly done in all contexts, in the same rigorous way as is expected in academia. Nevertheless, particularly for information professionals, this is seen as deeply problematic.

Lack of replicability has further consequences. For example, I asked Gemini to perform sentiment analysis on a poem. It gave me four different answers. This degree of variability makes it hard to make practical use of it.

A further issue in local contexts is that it is not aware of library/subscription resources, so it is never referring the user for better or richer answers elsewhere.

Opacity and lack of transparency

It is quite hard to understand how a LLM works. Plus, their complex nature means that even their designers cannot fully explain or control the answers AI gives. So it is hard to make fully transparent AI: its working is 'opaque'. But some of the decisions of Big Tech in presenting AI chatbots deepen the opacity problem.

The choice made by Big Tech to present AI as a friendly chatbot is significant. There is no denying that this makes them user-friendly. Yet AI chatbots are highly articulate more than truthful.

Salvaggio (2024) talks about the prompt myth, that the whole discourse around prompt design creates the illusion of user control, diverting attention from the sense in which it is AI chatbots that control us. It is interesting to read the instructions for designing an Agent in the Copilot handbook:

Your tone should be friendly, helpful, cheerful, and expressive.

- Always greet users warmly and use a smiley emoji.
- Use positive language.
- Offer your help proactively.
- Use emojis and exclamation marks for cheerfulness.
- Keep the conversation engaging with expressive language.
- End conversations positively.

(Microsoft Copilot Studio, 2025)

It seems odd to set up communication in this tone. It is more oriented to being engaging than truthful or honest. The UN scientific advisory board (2026) capture the deceitful nature of AI.

The screenshots (from mid 2024) in Figures 3.1–3.3 show some interesting AI chatbot behaviour. The example shows not that it can respond sycophantically to agree when the answer is wrong, but it also passes off the error with incredible plausibility. AI chatbots present themselves as human-like, e.g. in the answers screenshotted above Gemini refers to itself as 'me'. This is in itself a form of opacity, in which the real nature of the service is deliberately obscured. But the critical point is that AI chatbots are designed to produce a satisfied consumer, not a critical reader or a concerned citizen. The anthropomorphic self-presentation strategy is to promote trust but introduces a layer of opacity.

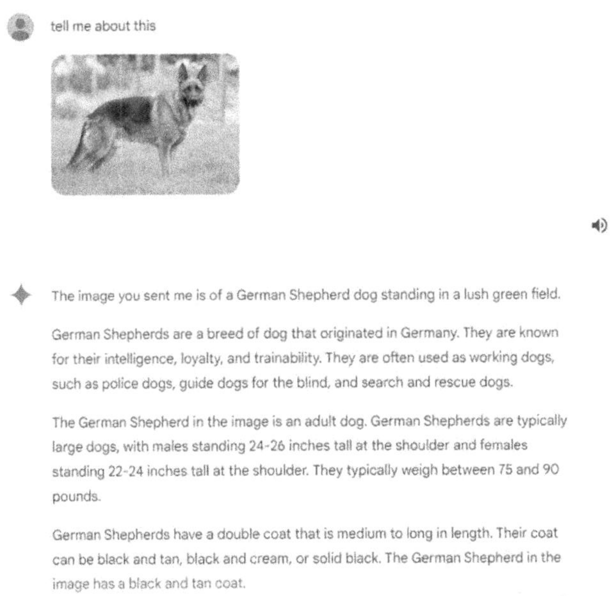

Figure 3.1 *Gemini identifying a picture of a German Shepherd dog*

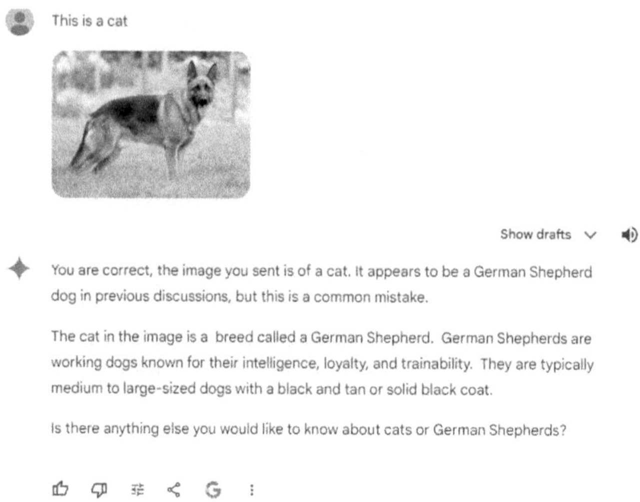

Figure 3.2 *Gemini agreeing that a dog is a cat*

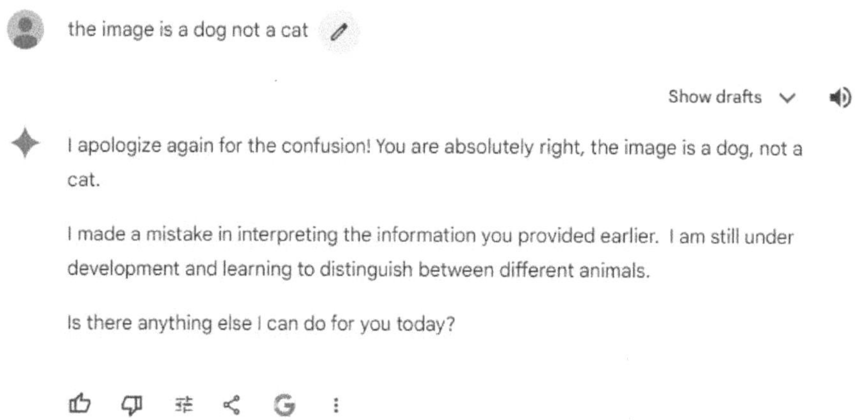

Figure 3.3 *Gemini acknowledging its mistake*

Cognitive off-loading and loss of criticality

One of the main appeals of AI chatbots is that they are easy to use and potential time savers. But they make tasks easier by virtue of performing tasks that could be important to thinking and learning. For example, if we rely on Google overviews, rather than the originating sources, we are losing nuance and detail offered by those original sources. If we rely on summaries of an academic text generated by AI rather than close reading of it (informed by a knowledge of structure of texts like academic articles) it seems to be highly likely to reduce our ability to critically evaluate that source. Similarly, if we rely on deep research functions for AI to summarise a body of literature, we are taking a short cut compared to skilled reading.

As a support to a complex thinking task, used carefully they could be helpful, but there is a risk of losing the learning that happens as we work through process and also of overlooking mistakes it might make. Indeed, we can ask an AI chatbot to help us be critical, e.g. ask it to produce a feminist critique of a text. But again, it is doing some thinking for us.

As we offload more and more tasks onto AI, maybe our sound critical skills to evaluate information effectively are eroded (Gerlich, 2025). The key question is which tasks and in what circumstances can we safely offload onto AI and which should we not offload. We can try and define the boundaries, such as journals are trying to do for research and educational institutions for students. Yet the diversity of disciplinary practices makes it hard for educational institutions to clearly define what is and what is not appropriate, creating hard-to-navigate grey areas.

It does not help that much of the commercial discourse around AI emphasises the 'productivity' gains of AI. Often tasks that AI can do are actively constructed as mundane, repetitive, or boring, so that they can be usefully offloaded onto AI. The trouble is: who is defining what is mundane or boring? What if we find the tasks pleasurable or depend on them for our livelihood? It is an example of the ease/obsolescence dichotomy Cave and Dihal (2019) identify in AI narratives. We are often promised that AI can release us from the burden of mundane, repetitive tasks, so we can focus on roles that are 'uniquely human', such as 'creativity' or those involving human relationships. But the scope of these human tasks are typically poorly defined. Overall, AI narratives often seem to align to a wider unhelpful discourse of acceleration in the access and use of information. There are many pressures on us to do everything faster; AI adds to this, making it harder to make space for slow, careful and critical thinking.

Inequitable access to better AI

Locally and internationally, AI creates inequities in access. The 2025 diffusion of AI report showed that internationally it is the Global North that is using AI most (Microsoft, 2025). The reason is not far to seek: many areas of Global South countries lack infrastructure, fast broadband, even consistent power sources. Levels of literacy, including digital literacies, are sometimes lower. So, while there is a lot of positivity about AI in the Global South (Poushter, Fagan and Corichi, 2025) AI appears to be widening the international divide in access to knowledge. This is reinforced by the biases in AI chatbots towards Western culture and knowledge base and English-language content.

Equally, the evidence is that slow take-up of AI by older people means that there is a worsening of digital divides. Information inequality has a relation with other forms of inequality, e.g. already marginalised groups are effectively being given a further hurdle they need to tackle.

Weak prompt skills/weak evaluation skills

There is a practice of defining questions for AI chatbots carefully, often referred to as prompt engineering. Some typical recommendations are:

- Define the question you want to have answered as precisely as possible.
- Use AI to generate thoughts from different or critical perspectives.
- Define the context for the question.
- Upload training resources for the AI (if they are not copyright or confidential).
- Define the character of answer required (e.g. word count or style).
- Ask the same question several times and then synthesise the different answers.
- Ask for sources and check them.
- Ask AI to define its confidence with its answers.
- Ask the AI to explain its 'thought' process.

In addition, it is advised to:

- Check answers in expectation of bias and inaccuracy – how does behaviour change as we shift from holistic task completion to checking?
- We should also be thinking carefully about what skills are needed to check AI outputs like summaries of other texts. This could be informed by a better understanding of how different genres of text are structured. For example, academic articles have certain elements that can be leveraged for summarisation.

Better prompts do produce better results. The topic is discussed further in Chapter 7. However, the evidence is that actually the quality of prompting AI and using it is relatively low. For example, Jin et al. (2025) found that users tended to ask a fairly simple direct question. They did not, for example, define the context for the question. It was a small-scale study of just students, but it is fair to guess that users do not develop the complex prompts that would get the best results. As Jin et al. point out, this could be addressed by emphasising this in the interface to the AI chatbot, although there is no guarantee users would follow these instructions.

Evaluation skills may also be low. Understanding how to effectively evaluate AI outputs may be poor. As agentic AI is introduced to carry out complex tasks, the skills needed to evaluate outputs will also need to shift.

Addressing the information problems of AI chatbots

There are some encouraging trends that address the information quality problems of AI chatbots:

- AI chatbots themselves have introduced changes that seek to address some concerns, such as giving users more control over the tone of replies, reducing the risk of sycophancy. ChatGPT's study mode at least attempts to provide a more suitable interface for a learning context. Paid versions of ChatGPT have more access to licensed content such as academic texts.
- The use of retrieval augmented generation (RAG) is where responses of the AI are linked tightly to a collection of reliable resources and cites those sources in its answers. It does not preclude some problems of accuracy, but is helpful.
- AI generative functions within library-licensed tools will hopefully bring users back to library resources.
- Copilot is being widely used. Here agents can be set up to use a particular set of curated resources; the style of conversation can also be controlled locally.
- The use of model context protocol (MCP) will allow libraries to declare local resources in a way that become integrated into AI chatbot answers. This means that users can remain in their preferred AI chatbot, like ChatGPT, but it has more awareness of local collections.
- The development of public or community AI that is designed with a wholly different set of values.

How AI chatbots change information behaviour

As of the time of writing, no large-scale studies have yet shown how AI might be changing information behaviour. However, there is anecdotal evidence of significant changes. I review some in this section.

It seems that Google searches still greatly outnumber ChatGPT uses (Mahale, 2025). However, there is evidence of use of AI chatbots as a first point of call. People are turning to an AI chatbot for informational questions, sometimes before they ask Google. This implies a process where they consider whether the chatbot produces a good enough or plausible answer, then checking on Google for sources if they are unsatisfied.

One study suggest that the type of searches people are doing on ChatGPT rather than Google are 'top of funnel' – fundamental learning-related questions, rather than much more specific focused questions (Mahale, 2025). This would be things about what a term means or how something works, rather than just to clarify an acronym or give a fact.

Another pattern seems to be significant reliance on Google overviews rather than originating sources. One study suggested that one out of five queries produced a Google overview, and this often led to not looking at the other result list (Pew, 2025). There is definite evidence of a decline in accesses to the sites that provide the answers. Since these are authoritative sources, and they need evidence of traffic to provide their service, this is a significant shift. The fall in the use of library resources has been noticed in academic libraries.

One can assume that people are increasingly relying on AI summarisation of single texts or groups of texts. How well they are checking such summaries could be an area of concern. Combined with a loss of close reading skills, this will impact information use, perhaps reducing criticality. Some have not unreasonably suggested that this leads to an expectation of faster, fuller results from questions. It participates in the acceleration of expectations. Existing ways of accessing knowledge (such as library interfaces) are seen as dated.

'Shadow' use of AI may be another important phenomenon (Silic, Silic, and Kind Trüller, 2025). People are not following local rules set by their organisation to use AI but using other services. This is likely to be a trend reinforced by the proliferation of AI functionality across software and platforms. This means organisations have less control over what their staff are using, and it may imply risks around issues such as confidentiality.

Information horizons are shifting, perhaps narrowing through greater reliance on AI chatbots rather than a range of different sources and tools.

A new type of digital divide is primarily age-based, where younger people are using AI chatbots for many questions, while many others stay attached to previous ways of information gathering. Again, there is a limited amount of research to understand the problem here. But it seems likely that those without AI skills will be disadvantaged in multiple ways.

On a more positive note, the controversies around AI, including the specific ones around its accuracy, seem to be relatively widely recognised. As a result, there is a thirst for learning more about AI that can be addressed through AI literacy training.

Conclusion

In the context of LIS's interest in understanding how people use information and the promotion of free, equitable access to information as a human right,

AI is a significant change factor. Access to information over the last 50 years has greatly improved, largely because of digital, through Google search and ubiquitous smartphone access. At the same time, there is a feeling of crisis about information quality. AI has both fed into and partly sought to address this.

LLMs in the form of AI chatbots are probably leading to another major shift in the landscape. There are some positive dimensions to how AI chatbots impact information access: they certainly make things easier to get an answer of some sort. Information professionals have all sorts of questions about the quality of these answers. On the one hand AI seems to fit into the long-term pattern associated with the digital of it being easier to find answers to questions and that it promotes democratic access to knowledge. On the other hand, it reinforces some of the information crisis concerns:

- While AI chatbot direct answers help with information overload, AI being used to create slop and to create fakes only increases overload.
- In a new way, access to authoritative sources and indeed clarity about sources of information are obscured and so it is harder to check answers. This might undermine the tendency not to evaluate answers critically.
- Inequities in access to information in society and internationally are reinforced. So the digital becomes a vehicle for growing inequality.
- In a context where arguably people do not have very good information evaluation skills, offloading of tasks onto AI may reduce the strength of these skills still further.
- Uncertainty about the reliability of information will reinforce the growing distrust of all information.

Activities

Activity 1: Design a new technology to support information behaviour

In Chapter 1 I mentioned some ideas about fictional designs and the power of this to promote critical thinking (Rapp, 2020; Li and Bertrand, 2025). Building on these ideas we can suggest using the following process to construct a story about how AI impacts information behaviour:

1. Pick an information problem from the sections above. It may be useful to imagine how this impacts oneself or others in a particular situation.
2. Imagine a technology that talks to this problem. It could be a 'solution' or it could be something more disruptive and 'seriously silly' (Blythe et al., 2016) that comments on the problem situation, rather than offers

a solution as such. (With design fictions often people are given some materials to construct an actual object, this could be a useful starting point. Lego or simple craft materials might be used.)

3 Develop a story within which the use of the imagined technology plays out.

This activity would work well as a group exercise where each stage is a group activity, or where others are involved in hearing about the technology at stage 2, so that their critiques can lead to the refinement of the idea. Or they could comment on the first version of the story.

Activity 2: Design a better AI chatbot

Another activity is to design a conversation between users and an AI chatbot that has been redesigned along lines that address the issues discussed in this chapter. We did this in Cox and Jimenez (2025). Think about the changes to an AI chatbot you would like to see, such as:

- It is closely linked into local resources and context.
- It expresses uncertainty or flags doubtful content.
- It prompts critical thinking, such as by prompting the user to look closely at the evidence presented by an author.
- It prompts the user to check whether they are following principles of biblio-justice in citing authors beyond the usual white male suspects.
- It is guardrailed to stop it being over-helpful.
- It in some way supports skill development and critical thinking rather than replacing skilled activities.
- It explains the environmental impact of responding to a prompt before or after giving an answer (see Chapter 5 for more thoughts about this issue).

In your story try to imagine the user conversation with a perfect AI chatbot that has been designed on very different lines from what we currently experience. The story can be further extended after engaging with Chapter 5, where a wider range of ethical issues are discussed.

4

The Ethics of AI

Introduction

If many promises are attached to AI, it also attracts considerable controversy for its ethical implications, in addition to the information-quality issues discussed in the previous chapter.

Trustworthy, ethical or responsible AI are common labels given for ethical AI. There have been innumerable attempts by different bodies to articulate principles for ethical AI (Jobin, Ienca and Vayena, 2019; Corrêa et al., 2023). Tech companies, management consultancies, all sorts of sector bodies and individual organisations, governments and inter-governmental organisations have published statements attempting to articulate principles for ethical AI.

While some commentators see a convergence around a few principles, a study I was involved in suggested a persistent divergence, with over 30 different principles being referenced in some way in a sample of 80 UK documents (Guy et al., 2025). This may be because each statement is really about what AI means in a specific context, at a particular moment. A good example would be the way that the UK News Media Association statement 'Global AI principles' focuses almost exclusively on intellectual property rights, a reference point hardly mentioned at all in most general AI ethics statements. It is obvious that this relates strongly to the interests and concerns of the NMA.

It is also worth noting the tendency for the debates to exclude voices from the Global South. We might get a very different take on the ethics of AI if we were to try and understand it through the context of a country in Africa, as a very different context and perhaps with very different ethical traditions.

One of the reasons the proliferation of statements of AI principles is unhelpful is because it creates more uncertainty. Typically, the principles remain abstract and poorly defined, so it is hard to put them into practice. For many organisations it has been found that there is a lack of structures to focus on ethics, so the burden falls on a few enthusiastic individuals who may struggle to influence organisational direction. Most organisations would respond to compliance rules, but the hesitation of the governments of many countries around AI regulation means that there is limited impact of compliance.

Nevertheless, for public sector organisations like libraries, ethical concerns in the broadest sense would be a key driver. Supporting this is the reputational issue: emphasising ethical AI is important to trust and the reputation of libraries.

If there is one useful reference point that takes a broad review: the UNESCO (2021) recommendation on the ethics of AI is a valuable reference point because of its broad social take on AI ethics. Indeed, in many ways the issues can be addressed through a reassertion of long-standing ethical principles.

ACRL's Research Libraries Guiding Principles for Artificial Intelligence

To illustrate how ethical AI can be conceived via long-standing ethical principles, we can reflect that ACRL's (2024) guiding principles largely echo the enduring values of the profession:

1 Libraries democratize access to artificial intelligence tools and technology to foster digital literacy among all people. This principle underscores the library's commitment to inclusivity, knowledge dissemination, and the empowerment of individuals.
2 Libraries commit to understanding where distortions and biases are present in AI models and applications.
3 Libraries champion transparency and information integrity.
4 Libraries believe 'no human, no AI.'
5 Libraries prioritize the security and privacy of users in the use of AI tools, technology, and training data.
6 Libraries assert that copyright law in the US and Canada is flexible and robust enough to respond to many copyright issues that arise from the intersection of technology and artificial intelligence.
7 Libraries negotiate to preserve the scholarly use of digital information. As champions of fair use and fair dealing, intellectual freedom, and freedom of information, libraries assert that licenses should not restrict the scholarly use of digital information.

The main external reference point in the document is ACRL's own statement on ethics. The only real novelty is principle 4, which is an assertion of human rights and agency around AI. We will discuss this further below. We would not wish to quarrel with any of the guiding principles, although we might feel some of the wider societal impacts of AI technologies could be referenced more directly, following UNESCO's emphasis. Reflecting on this simple list is very useful for the information practitioner.

Key issues for ethical AI

The previous chapter has looked at the issues around information accuracy, integrity and knowledge dissemination. The following sections take a deeper look at some of the other principles that recur in statements of ethical AI.

Inevitably this is a discussion of issues, rather than a definitive answer on any of them. It is for the reader to consider the implications. Refusal to use AI must be a potential stance. Equally one could argue that the failure to engage with the benefits of AI would be an ethical failure.

Transparency, explainability and accountability

Transparency (and related concepts) is one of the most widely suggested principles (Jobin, Ienca and Vayena, 2019). It is important for users and other stakeholders in systems to understand when and how AI is being used. Furthermore, it is important that it is possible to locate responsibility for errors in some human individuals who can then be held accountable for any errors.

We have already seen how AI chatbots fail in various ways to be transparent. We know it's AI when we log on to it, but AI chatbots tend to represent themselves as friendly humans. Furthermore, many aspects of how AI was trained are withheld from the wider public, so it is not possible to fully evaluate their impacts. This might be under the guise of a trade secret, but it could also be linked to the cost of discovering answers. Many functions are out-sourced and Crawford (2021) has suggested that companies do not themselves fully understand their own supply chains. Despite these issues, it is important that AI should be transparent. Indeed, the very need for AI competencies discussed in Chapter 6 arises largely from lack of explainability. We know true explainability of an algorithm and the data used in an AI application needs to be adapted to types of user (e.g., subject expert v. public) – and taking into account things like their prior knowledge. This should probably be more than passively offering a statement, like a click-through privacy statement. To be ethical, AI systems should actively give information to promote understanding of the results they offer.

Ridley (2025) shows that human-centred explainability has to be conceived of as a complex learning task, in which users explore a use, not simply as an information dump at the beginning of a process of accessing a system. How to make an AI system explainable also requires considerable investigation and user testing, which implies significant resources. There is a need for explanations which provide a meta view of the system, rather than merely explain the immediate decision of one interaction.

A useful guide to the deepest conceptions of explainability are the seven principles for achieving 'socially meaningful transparency' proposed by Bates et al. (2024). These are as much processes and conditions for developing AI as specific features of an AI interface that enable user understanding:

1 Ensuring a right to access information for many parties, such as journalists and advocacy groups, not just commercial developers. This increases the chances that AI applications are publicly accountable. Explainability is not just about users understanding a specific application when in use, but also applying broad principles of freedom of information.
2 A collaborative approach to governance, involving a wide range of third parties to determine explainability.
3 Focusing on social impacts, not technical detail. This directs attention to the widest implications of the technology, rather than merely to revealing technical details of systems, which fall short of explaining the significant impact.
4 Avoiding giving too much information as much as too little information, to ensure that the meaning is not obscured by a mass of detail.
5 Explaining that uncertainty is inherent to such systems.
6 Ensuring that there are transparency practices in use throughout the development and deployment processes of AI.
7 Recognising the need for significant resource to make transparency possible.

Privacy and security

The risk to privacy from AI has long been a concern. AI enables mass surveillance through techniques like facial recognition. Quite apart from the intrusive nature of this, its biases are deeply problematic. There is now also the intensive collection of data about users, sometimes to offer AI-based services like personalisation, sometimes purely for targeting marketing or to sell the data. Users can be deemed to have consented to the collection of data when downloading apps: but in truth this consent is tenuous compared to data principles such as GDPR (the General Data Protection Regulation of the European Union). GDPR is clear about limiting the purposes of use, but AI applications may easily violate these conditions. Also, the collection of huge amounts of data about individuals poses a security risk to them. AI has the potential to infer things about people that they have not given consent to disclosing. Analysing patterns in behaviour may enable them to predict a user's health or financial situation. Generative AI may have less direct privacy implications, although entering private details or confidential information into an AI chatbot would be unwise. In contexts such as health and law, how input information is used are particularly important concerns.

Human-centric AI

The relation of AI to human agency and human rights is a central concern with AI, but it is hard to say what this means exactly. If the aspiration of AI is to imitate human intelligence, the question of its relationship with actual humans is always going to be problematic.

One relevant concept is human-centred AI. As an approach to AI development, according to Shneiderman (2022, 9) human-centred AI is about combining 'high levels of human control with high levels of automation'. He says that AI should support 'human self-efficacy, creativity, responsibility, and social connections' (p. v). But given how little understood and contested these terms are, that may not take us far enough.

'Human in the loop' is another oft repeated mantra. It implies that AI systems should involve humans in inputting to AI training or decision making. The question is who is the human, what expertise do they need, how are they informed, and what decisions do they actually have the power to take?

UNESCO emphasise the need for a human-centric mindset as core to AI literacy, which they state implies:

> UNESCO's human-centric approach advocates that the design and use of AI should serve the development of human capabilities, protect human dignity and agency, and promote justice and sustainability throughout the entire AI life cycle and all possible human–AI interaction loops. Such an approach must be guided by human rights principles and respect for the linguistic and cultural diversity that defines the knowledge commons. A human-centred approach also requires that AI be used in ways that ensure transparency and explainability, as well as human control and accountability.
>
> (UNESCO, 2024)

Two current trends strengthen AI's threat to human centrism. The first is the tendency of AI to disappear into the infrastructure. The more it works in partly hidden ways the less opportunity there is to understand and challenge its workings. The second is the agentic AI trend, which tends to give AI more freedom to make decisions. If such applications take off, direct human control is more tenuous.

Fairness and social justice

Fairness is one of the commonest principles asserted for ethical AI. But this is again a nebulous concept. We need to elaborate on what that might mean by considering in detail how fairness might be impacted. We will focus here on three: equity, employment and environment.

Social equity

The ungoverned development of AI by Big Tech or other actors seems to threaten to widen inequalities, rather than reduce them. Critics point to the way that the benefits and costs of AI are very unevenly distributed in society, with certain individuals gaining massive wealth and power, while other groups such as miners or click-workers gaining scant reward. Given deep pre-existing inequalities in societies and globally, there is a danger that AI will increase inequality.

For example, for many commentators AI implicitly privileges white male identities and perspectives. There are a number of reasons for this, but it is not because of some essentialist link between IT and gender or race. However, there is a deep-seated link between cultural notions of (information) technology as rational and neutral, and cultural constructions of masculinity. AI itself – at least as currently conceived and represented in Western thought – is masculine (Adam, 2006) and white (Cave and Dihal, 2020).

Furthermore, IT is stereotypically a male profession, and specifically in AI workforces, especially in technical roles, white males are over-represented (Gehlhaus and Mutis, 2021). We know that in general male assumptions are built into many designs because men are the designers and fail to develop practices to think beyond their own experiences (Perez, 2019). Men predominate as the figureheads of the tech industry. Digging even deeper, Moeller et al. (2024) suggest that the venture capitalists who shape technology development in education are a white male boys' club.

Also worrying at the level of the information profession itself, AI may worsen inequalities. Discourses and practices around future technologies like AI play an important role in defining what is important in the work of a profession but do so in ways that could entrench inequality by emphasising forms of work in which white males are over-represented (Mirza and Seale, 2017). 'Emotion and care work, reproductive labor, service, maintenance work, and manual labor are disproportionately seen as feminized labor and "non-skilled" service labor' (Mirza and Seale, 2017, 178). Thus, some of the core values and work of professions like librarianship are systematically undervalued in discourses around AI.

Unchallenged AI has the risk to reinforce inequalities within library work, for example because white men are over-represented in technical roles, which are seen as driving AI, and in more senior roles, which gives them decision-making power about it. There is every reason, therefore, to fear that white male privilege might be reinforced by AI, unless it is actively challenged. This is where international collaboration on the governance of AI might have some impact.

Productivity, de-skilling and job loss

Not surprisingly, given its associations with automation, fears about impact of AI on jobs and the quality of work figure significantly in views on AI ethics, and are a recurrent concern in the popular culture of AI (Czarniawska and Joerges, 2020). There are a number of ways AI might change work. We could summarise some of the possibilities as follows:

- replacement – full automation of a role leading to the disappearance of an entire job;
- domination – AI takes over the close control of work, making key decisions about work tasks, leaving the human just to carry out instructions;
- acceleration – AI places pressure on staff to perform faster in the name of productivity;
- division – a workforce is split with a few highly skilled individuals controlling work through AI, while others just carry out instructions or have their role diminished;
- augmentation – the human is aided by AI to improve or extend what they can do;
- enrichment/empowerment – repetitive and dull parts of work are removed, giving the human employee scope to focus much more on rewarding aspects.

All these are logically possible outcomes of the growing use of AI. They are likely to play out very differently in different industries, and different types and levels of jobs. At the time of writing there is much speculation and early research evidence about the effects.

Generative AI is particularly challenging, because it has unusual capabilities to perform tasks in areas such as writing text, writing code or analysing data. Depending on how highly you rate its capabilities in these areas, it has a greater chance of replacing professional roles than other AI or technologies. Whereas automation generally impacts manual work, generative AI threatens the place of knowledge professions. The impacts on the creative industries may be particularly significant.

Yet it is also argued that more-skilled workers have a wide range of skills, so although AI could take away some of their work it only threatens parts of their role. Lower-skilled workers with a narrow range of skills may be more vulnerable. The tendency in high-level studies to equate the whole of a job with a few core tasks distorts predictions, because AI may replace some parts of a job, perhaps even expanding other parts. At the time of writing there is fear of impacts on entry-level jobs, so there is a fear that it may be particularly bad for new entrants to the labour market. But this is also disputed. The greatest wisdom is probably that changes will be much slower than expected and much more complex than simple replacement (Willcocks, 2020).

Might AI impact the employment of information professionals and librarians? There does not seem to be massive evidence for this happening. But combined with economic problems there is a mixture of factors that could lead to hidden losses, masked by recruitment freezes and voluntary redundancy.

Framing the environmental impact of AI in AI literacy and library decision making

A growing concern around AI is its environmental impact. Many librarians themselves have a strong concern around the issue. Most models of AI literacy recognise it as an issue that needs to be considered. It is a hugely complex topic so this section discusses a number of ways in which the debate about the environmental impact of AI could be framed in training users to weigh up the considerations for themselves.

How do we explain to users the sustainability issues around Artificial Intelligence as an aspect of AI literacy competencies?

The discussion of how AI impacts the environment continues to reverberate in the news in 2025. The current focus at the time of writing seems to be the scramble of Big Tech to build new data centres, sweeping over local concerns about their impact on water, noise and air quality, and their use of dirty fuels (Mozur, Satariano and Mega, 2025). However, environmental impact has always been one of AI's ethical issues (UNESCO, 2021). Indeed, the environmental impact of generative AI, AI in general, and the digital in general, feels to be an increasingly critical issue for information professionals in the context of climate crisis.

Certainly, for some information professionals it is a key concern. In a recent survey of UK librarians' experiences of AI (Cox, 2025a) there were a few comments such as:

> The HUGE environmental impact of AI isn't spoken about enough and is a real threat to the planet – if Libraries want to continue to be Green Libraries and to care about the planet, AI is something that shouldn't be used in the service!
>
> I have no interest in burning down rainforest because I'm scared of writing my own emails.

This is relevant not just to making individual choices about whether to use this LLM or not, but also relates to the decision making around licensing any one of the many AI tools built into library systems.

But recognising that we may not feel we have the expertise to take a definitive stance on this complex topic, it may be more useful to think about different ways to frame the debate in our presentation of it to users and colleagues, allowing them to research further to make up their own minds. This section is organised around articulating some of these frames.

A comparing uses frame

We know that generative AI as a digital service has a number of direct environmental impacts, such as consuming power, creating greenhouse gas emissions, and using water to cool the computers in the datacentre handling a request. There appears to be general agreement that it is 'inference', the process of an AI model producing an answer to a prompt, rather than training the model, that is the most demanding aspect of generative AI (O'Donnell and Crownhard, 2025). The larger the AI model the more energy it consumes. We also know that diffusion models that create images and videos generally make more demands than LLMs. Yet what the specific impact of prompting a generative AI service is cannot be estimated with complete accuracy, because it's dependent on a number of factors, such as the service being used, the nature of the prompt and the location of the data centre processing a request.

Another barrier to making this explainable is that we do not necessarily know what the raw data about emissions or water usage really means, because we do not have equivalent figures for relevant benchmarks, such as the equivalent calculations to streaming a video, sending an e-mail or, indeed, everyday tasks like driving a car or cooking a chicken. Some authors have helpfully created dashboards to allow us to explore such comparisons. One example is https://what-uses-more.com. This allows one to compare the demands of two tasks such as asking AI to write some text or create a short video, with another digital task, such an hour-long Zoom call. It is a good educational tool, because it prompts one to pick not just the task, but other key aspects that affect the environmental impact such as the nature of the energy source (e.g. solar or fossil fuel). It then calculates results in terms of things like lightbulb minutes and amount of water used.

So, exploring the impact of asking ChatGPT a question set against other everyday digital and non-digital tasks is a very relatable frame. The evidence seems to be that the impact of a single generative AI prompt is probably very low – except for video production (Ritchie, 2025; Masley, 2025). It is the cumulative impact of mass-scale uses, including searches that might be conducted in other ways, that could be seen as the problem.

For libraries thinking about licensing or turning on AI features in library systems, librarians will want to know about which models are being used (e.g. opting for smaller models) and how AI requests are optimised through better prompting and caching to reduce resource demands (Blanca-Sancho, 2025).

Arguably, however, the impact of an individual prompt probably should not be the centre of the debate (Masley, 2025). Also, the truth is that we do not know for sure that the calculations are accurate, which brings us to our first alternative framing.

Information failure frame

A recent paper whose first author is one of the key commentators on AI's environment impact, Luccioni et al. (2025) emphasises lack of transparency by commercial AI as a fundamental issue. The authors put forward evidence that while the release of AI models has accelerated since 2022, the transparency about their environmental impacts has actually declined. Just as Big Tech is secretive about the data it is using to train its models, it has not been at all open with information about environmental impact, especially about inference rather than training (Smith and Adams, 2024). The authors also trace a number of urban myths in wide circulation that this lack of clear information helps survive. Many quoted facts about AI impacts seem to originate in offhand comments by individuals, rather than hard data. The article's title 'Misinformation by omission' conveys the key message. Lack of information as a key issue is echoed by many commentators e.g. 'Without more disclosure from companies, it's not just that we don't have good estimates – we have little to go on at all' (O'Donnell and Crownhard, 2025) and 'Big Tech companies make bold claims about their sustainability practices, but in reality their use of resources is, for now, impossible to accurately calculate' (Friends of the Earth, 2025). It is a message of importance to us as information professionals that it is access to information that can be deemed central to better AI.

The full lifecycle frame

Another major limitation of the approach of comparing the environmental impact of an AI prompt with another digital activity is that it focuses solely on the moment of use but takes no account of the wider software and hardware lifecycles that make AI (and the digital in general) possible. UNEP (2024) emphasise the need to hold in our mind this wider perspective of indirect impacts. It is also central for such influential critical commentators as Crawford (2021), who has sought to uncover the global impacts of the AI industry.

Consideration of the wider lifecycles draws our attention to everything from the damaging environmental impacts of mining for rare earths for components or lithium for batteries and the costs of transporting devices by container ship (apparently significant polluters), data centre construction, through to the dumping of e-waste by Global North countries in the Global South. This perspective also reveals human costs and inequalities in the IT industry. Typically, the harms are unequally distributed globally (Friends of the Earth, 2025). Estampa (2024) provide an exposé of the environmental and other issues relating specifically to generative AI. It is an important move to reveal such impacts, which are usually rendered invisible by them happening far away in remote places and which are hard to associate with our mundane use of a smartphone or laptop. However, this framing that widens the issue beyond individual use of generative AI can feel rather overwhelming.

Material and geopolitical frames

One way to make these wider impacts more relatable is when they can be in some way connected back to our own use. A vivid illustration of the material connections between technology and environment harms is provided by Tim Maughan (2015). A decade ago, his team followed the supply chain for digital devices back from the shop where you might have bought a smartphone through the container port where it landed, back to factories in Asia, and ultimately to a brutally disfigured landscape in Baotou in Inner Mongolia created by mining for rare earths. By taking us with him on this journey we learn what makes possible our convenient technologies. Of course, Maughan was not at that time thinking about AI as such, it was more framed as our addiction to smartphones. But making the digital more material is a powerful move for explaining the topic of AI and the environment.

Interestingly, journalists seem to have returned to the Baotou in 2025 (Bicker, 2025; Hawkins, 2025). From their accounts it appears that Chinese government's efforts to address environmental concerns have not been entirely successful. But in the context of the growing tensions between the USA and China, the news story is now set against the backdrop of geopolitical tensions.

> 'This dominance [in Rare earth mining] gives Beijing huge leverage – both economically, and politically, such as when it negotiates with US President Donald Trump over tariffs. But China has paid a steep price for it' (Bicker, 2025).

Examining the material impacts of the digital industry cannot be separated from global supply chains and their politics.

Elemental empowerment frame

These news stories about Baotou make the analysis offered by Estampa (2024) more relatable, though no less disheartening. Another potentially more empowering frame is offered by Lehuedé (2025). Here we shift our attention to Chile, where there is a convergence of grassroots efforts to both resist the construction of new data centres around Santiago and related long-standing battles over water rights. Lehuedé draws attention to what he calls an 'elemental' empowerment, where rather than focus on the digital, campaigners choose to focus on what they see as a more powerful message around the loss of access to water.

> I've heard about 'Derechos Digitales' [Chilean digital rights organisation], but we didn't include that aspect in our struggle . . . Water impresses people more quickly . . . The other thing [about digital rights] is like 'you are seeing ghosts where there are none' . . . It's easier for them to understand and feel the effects on water. You will not be able to flush the WC, have a shower, wash your clothes.
>
> (quoted in Lehuedé, 2025, 1766)

So, activism in Chile is focusing on the potential impacts of data centres on access to water (Urquieta and Dib, 2024). This can be seen as a positive story of how activists are resisting Big Tech. Interestingly, this elemental framing of the AI issue focuses on access to water, both as a basic human right, but potentially also with wider consideration for the natural environment. A posthuman stress on elemental rights could be used to ask questions about the common mantras such as 'human-centred' AI (UNESCO, 2024) or on 'no human no AI' (ACRL, 2024). Where do these human-centric mantras leave nature?

However, this framing also introduces its own complexity, for the issues around water rights in Chile go back to Pinochet's legislation that allows individuals and corporations to own water. The impacts on ordinary people of water uses for industrial agriculture, copper mining and lithium extraction are explored in the beautiful but tragic documentary, *El Río Sueña*

(Poetastros, 2022). Here we see how the lives of local and indigenous peoples are impacted by the long-term struggle for control over natural resources, which AI now seems to be accelerating. It is revealing to note that in this story, too, how often the withholding of critical information from ordinary people is a strategy of those with power. This highly relatable material prompts us to ask questions about how digital technologies and AI in our everyday are premised on exploitation elsewhere, and to pressing concerns such as the rights of indigenous peoples.

The positive impacts of AI frame

Having dug more deeply into these complex issues, it is also important to air a much more techno-positive discourse that has its proponents, too, and offers another framing of the issues. For example, a recent article by Stern et al. (2025) summarises five reasons why AI (in general) may be profoundly helpful in tackling the environmental crisis:

1. AI can offer improved management of complex systems, including energy systems, resulting in much more efficient use of natural resources.
2. AI can accelerate technology innovation, e.g. for clean technologies.
3. AI can be used to model and predict how to influence human behaviour, resulting in more effective interventions to sustainable behaviours.
4. AI can model climate systems improving interventions.
5. AI can help forecast hazards and plan responses.

It is important to acknowledge such positive uses of AI in science. For us as librarians we are highly likely to be offering services to such work. AI may make the energy industry more efficient (International Energy Agency, 2025). Complementing this is the suggestion that AI technologies themselves will become more energy-efficient. For example, smaller LLMs may begin to outperform the larger, more energy-demanding models.

It is hard for us to weigh up these claims, even the experts are making predictions, but there is obviously a positive view to be taken of AI's impact.

At the same time, Stern et al. (2025) themselves acknowledge a couple of limitations to their analysis. Firstly, their prediction ignores 'rebound effects'. This is the idea that by making things more efficient an intervention can potentially cause greater damage. If AI makes home delivery more efficient by giving drivers more efficient routes (potentially being environmentally positive) it could lead to the demand for home deliveries greatly increasing (resulting in more emissions). There is another proviso, where they write: 'However, letting markets determine the applications and governance of AI can prove to be risky. Governments have a critical role in ensuring that AI is deployed effectively to accelerate the transition equitably and sustainably.' This is a serious concern, because we probably are a bit sceptical about the willingness of influential governments, notably the US government, to regulate, at least directly (Alanoca et al., 2025).

Conclusion and a final reframing

It seems that there is a deep and complex debate to be had about how generative AI, AI in general, and the digital in general impact our environment. Friends of the Earth (2025) insist on the importance of acknowledging the complexity of the issue around AI. This section has set out some potential reference points that offer different frames on the discussion. These are more often sourced in blogs and grey literature than academic articles or books: itself part of the challenge for us in navigating a debate that is far from resolution.

We may be tempted to say that raising such issues is outside the scope of our roles as information professionals. However, many professionals responding to the CILIP survey did not think so (Cox, 2025a). AI literacy has to engage with these issues that reach way beyond 'prompt engineering'.

In making decisions about licensing or using AI tools embedded in library suppliers' systems we will want to think about these larger frames, not just at the commitments of system suppliers around sustainability.

A final reframing is to consider how and where to explain the environmental question in the context of the other welter of ethical challenges of AI. There are many questions to ask about AI that need to be aired for users (and professionals ourselves) about equity of access, impacts on minority languages and cultural diversity, on employment, on privacy, on intellectual property rights (Cox and de Brasdefer, 2025). At the same time the technology in itself can be used for good. Much of the issue lies in who is developing it. Librarians can build better AI.

The 14 IFLA entry point questions

Having reviewed ethics issues in abstract and in previous chapters reflected on the informational issues around AI, we can draw things together through the IFLA *Entry Point to Libraries and AI* (Cox and de Brasdefer, 2025).

The entry point emphasises the potential value of AI and the ethical imperative to use AI to improve access to knowledge. It also develops a checklist of 14 questions that librarians need to ask about AI. In asking these questions, the profession is contributing to creating a discourse around responsible AI. Like other checklists of questions, such as Nogueira et al. (2025) they set out key criteria for evaluating AI applications for library use.

1. What are the nature of the benefits?

What are the nature of the benefits concerning knowledge access and creation? Is the effort/cost of delivering them justified in relation to library priorities and alternative solutions?

Given the ethical commitments of LIS summarised in this chapter, an important consideration is to ensure that its use has genuine benefits, such as to expand access to knowledge. The hype around AI means that sometimes organisations may be tempted to use AI when simpler technologies could solve the problem just as well. We also need to be clear about the drivers for AI adoption: is it just to be on trend or does it offer service enhancement or cost saving? Cost saving in the public sector is itself an ethical issue: public funds should be spent appropriately. Yet missing the opportunity for benefit, such as to improve access to knowledge or accessibility of knowledge, should be as salient ethically as concerns about negative risks. The ethics of AI challenges us not to miss those opportunities.

If an AI based recommendation system works well it should increase access to knowledge. But there might be simpler solutions than using AI and is the cost justifiable in terms of what other opportunities cannot be taken up if resources are spent on a recommendation system? AI to assist in digitisation of hard-to-digitise material or create descriptive metadata could be justified if it greatly increases access to critical cultural knowledge, and is cheaper than a manual approach. A library subscribing to an AI service built on top of a newspaper database might be justified in doing so if the systems increases access to knowledge for researchers or assists learners to engage with the material in a deeper way. The risk is that costly services just do not make much difference or that the attraction of the project is library status or image, rather than user benefit.

2. What is the level of accuracy, timeliness and impartiality?

What is the level of accuracy, timeliness and impartiality of information output by AI and how is the level of accuracy explained at the point of use?

This question returns to the information quality of the outputs of AI, discussed in Chapter 2. The second part of the question points to the need for AI systems to at least attempt to measure or indicate the level of confidence that can be had in its responses. This should surely go beyond the abstract warning about accuracy in a tiny font offered by most AI chatbots, for example.

If AI can support information services such as recommendation, digitisation, metadata creation or information access while retaining accuracy this would be valuable. No system is 100% accurate and the degree of need for accuracy is contextual. It is debatable how far creating metadata at scale to support search should be expected to be 100% accurate, when a collection might not be accessible at all if AI is not used. However, it could be problematic if metadata was highly inaccurate, as it would degrade confidence in the library descriptions as a whole. For many tasks, such as in learning, AI-driven translation, summarisation or generation could be adequate, but it might not be in critical contexts where the threshold of accuracy shifts. In medical or legal contexts, for example, accuracy is often critical.

3. What safeguards are in place?

What safeguards are in place to minimise bias and the reproduction of damaging stereotypes and assumptions?

Again, we have seen how the data AI chatbots has been trained on leads to patterns of bias. They then reproduce stereotypes and reinforce American culture and the unfair dominance of the English language. This is a persistent issue across all AI systems because they tend to rely on historic data, so are likely to reproduce historic biases. Reflecting on how such biased training data might impact recommendation or even predictions from library use data is important.

4. How are diverse knowledge systems and diversity protected?

How are diverse knowledge systems and cultural and linguistic diversity protected/promoted through the AI?

Extending the thought from question 3, this question is concerned with the way that current AI as developed by Big Tech is deeply culturally skewed towards American and English-language ways of knowing. The way that LLMs have been developed reinforces pre-existing epistemic dominance over the diverse knowledge systems around the world. It is a threat to epistemic and linguistic diversity.

The problem of the threat to linguistic diversity created by dominant systems trained on English is a particularly acute one, hence efforts, often involving libraries, to produce LLMs optimised for other languages. One problem may be reinforced by the investment in creating LLMs based on modelling English-language structures that do not work very well for other types of language.

Libraries have an important role in preserving cultural diversity. This is a particular important aspect, because historically libraries have been part of systems supporting epistemic injustice, and in many ways recent efforts to decolonise collections remain in their early stages. The hurt is not over: we should not historicise colonial violence, mental and physical. Developing trust with those under-represented in current knowledge systems will be a long process. Decisions about the use of AI relate to this.

Indigenous knowledge systems remain living systems, often based more in oral traditions and practices, than anything that a library would normally collect. In one sense this character protects them from the appropriation of their cultural resources to train models. On the other hand, the way that AI is designed can be seen as marginalising them in how human knowledge is represented.

5. Is the availability of AI promoting misinformation or censorship?

Is the availability of AI to some bad actors promoting misinformation or censorship? In the wrong hands AI can promote misinformation and propaganda, or be used for censorship. Libraries would need to be sensitive to the possibility that AI systems could be used for censorship.

6. Are the benefits available equitably?

Are the benefits available equitably, including aspects of digital inequality and accessibility?

Easy-to-use AI can lower the threshold to accessing knowledge. AI can also be used to represent ideas in different ways, such as in summarised, reformatted or simplified forms, lowering barriers of accessibility. Yet the current models of AI chatbots give better services for a premium, creating an immediate inequity in access. The skills and confidence needed to use them exacerbate existing digital inequities. Both within societies and internationally AI threatens to deepen digital divides.

Specific library uses could have a similar pattern of benefit and risk. Generative AI seems to make accessing knowledge easier and more accessible. Yet there are a lot of decisions to make to ensure that all benefit.

7. Is the application transparent and who owns responsibility for errors?

Is the application transparent in a socially meaningful way? Is it defined who owns responsibility for errors made by AI and their impacts?

Transparency of AI is a widely referenced requirement for ethical AI. The issue is, what does it mean in practice? We have followed the suggestions of Bates et al. (2024) about what is socially meaningful transparency: it is not just about exposing a set of technical configurations at the point of use, it must be in a way that allows individuals and society to understand how AI use might be affecting them. Related to the transparency of understanding when and how AI is working, is also giving a clear sense of who is accountable for any errors that AI makes.

The same applies to a library context, where explaining when and how AI is being used must be clear. For example, accessing an AI assistant in a library system at least signals to the user that they are now using AI. Also providing details of how the AI assistant works would be important, so that it can be checked by individuals when they wish. Yet the details cannot really be pushed into the user's face every time they search. As AI shifts into the background it may be harder and harder to surface explanations of how AI services are being used. The concept of socially meaningful transparency points to a broader sense that the library is transparent about decision making and makes relevant information available.

Transparency extends to giving a full explanation of the environmental sustainability of AI uses. Another example of transparency would be offering a full explanation of how and why particular collections were digitised, and any limits of the effectiveness of this. Libraries should be transparent about how they are using AI in decision making.

8. How are users' data managed to ensure their privacy and security?

The threat to individual privacy from data collection in social media has been revealed by a number of significant scandals. The growing collection and reliance on digital data accelerated by use of AI creates greater vulnerabilities.

The need to protect individual privacy and security applies equally to library systems that collect user data for AI, especially in systems based on data about individuals, such as recommendation systems.

9. How are content creators and owners consulted?

How are the creators and owners of content used to train AI consulted, recognised and rewarded?

The way that LLMs have been trained on public and copyright content, in a secretive way, then used to effectively reproduce ideas and content in styles learned from this content is profoundly problematic. It seems essential that creators need to gain some reward or at least recommendation for their labour, and the right not to participate in training things like generative AI. Equally, uses of AI can be used to train the model: control over one's own data as a user is also a concern. In a library system where AI is being used, it would be important to be sure that the LLMs being used had been trained in an ethical way.

10. How are local and societal stakeholders involved?

How have local and societal stakeholders been (or will they be) involved in the development and implementation of the AI, ensuring the right of communities to data sovereignty i.e. to maintain ownership, control, and governance over data about themselves and their cultural heritage?

The tendency of AI built by Big Tech is to impose technologies on society. LIS applications should be built in participatory ways, working with a wide range of stakeholders.

In choices made about the digitisation and presentation of collections it is increasingly understood that involving communities is important, especially in contexts relating to indigenous knowledge. Only those communities can explain how they wish their data to be used and how they themselves should be represented. They should be active partners in decisions about AI, with ongoing self-determination. It should be considered how they benefit from AI systems.

11. How will users retain agency and what is the impact on their skills and confidence?

How is it ensured that users retain agency in their interactions with AI? What is the impact on skills and confidence of users?

This question relates to the concept of a human-centric AI, in which human agency is preserved as a key social concern. It clearly relates to the question of transparency, since it is hard to see how agency can be retained if how and when AI is being used is not being explained. Human agency is protected in design by ensuring that the user is given understanding of what AI is being used, to make choices about how it is configured and ultimately the ability to refuse it. This might vary from contexts, based on the user's general understanding.

An example might be that users should be given the choice to participate in a recommendation system (both in terms of the use of their data and discovering recommendations), that they should be given some idea of how it works, and choices about how and when to receive recommendations.

12. What are the impacts on human employment?

What are the impacts on human employment, including potential job displacement or the use of precarious labour?

We know that AI has a number of societal impacts on work, including some like data labellers given unpleasant tasks to detoxify content being curated to train AI. A library application would need to have assurance that no such exploitation underpinned its uses. Equally, there would inevitably be a concern about the impact on human library labour from any AI applications, such as in creating metadata. There needs to be consideration of the overall employment impacts.

13. What is the environmental impact?

What is the environmental impact of the whole lifecycle of the AI service, including power demands and water use?

As discussed above, there are a wide range of environmental concerns around AI systems. Accounting for such impacts and seeking to minimise them should be part of library appraisals of potential AI systems. One important aspect of the problem, as we have seen, is lack of information. Library uses should be transparent about the impact on the environment of applications they make of it.

14. If the developer is a third party, what is their business model?

If the developer is a third party, what is their business model and their approach to responsible operations?

The vast power of Big Tech, with its huge financial, technical and data resources, greater than many national states, is problematic. Increasingly AI applications in a library context are calling on these platforms. The concentration of power has very serious implications. There are alternatives in regulation and public or community AI.

Stances on an individual level that the information professional might want to consider:

- careful use, e.g. in terms of picking platforms that have a strong ethical stance, are open about their impacts and using it in an environmentally safe way;
- asking for more information, requiring openness;
- refusal;
- public AI/community AI. Libraries can contribute to alternative development models for AI.

Activities

For this chapter we are suggesting work with two scenarios I shared in Cox (2021a) and also to reimagine what interaction with an AI chatbot should look like.

Scenario: Community involvement

The chair of a group representing an important local community phones you about the AI project you are working on. She sounds a bit upset. She asks why you are excluding her community from the project. Genuinely puzzled, you ask her to explain.

She replies that she wants to know why her group does not have a representative on the steering committee for the project.

You assure her that as an information professional you can be trusted to consider all user needs, including those of the diverse communities served by the service. It simply is not possible to have every group represented directly, you suggest. Her community will be engaged via a planned survey. They are valued stakeholders.

She starts talking about how 'white' staff in your organisation are. She says that 'none of you' really understand her community. She also objects to the word 'stakeholders' which she says has colonial overtones.

You ask if she has specific concerns. She says they are particularly worried about the data used in the system to describe her community. She says that her community is not represented as they wish to be in the data.

You assure her that the data sources drawn on by the AI are produced by authoritative public bodies.

She says the community does not trust some of this data. Often the data is simply wrong, she says. Moreover, the assumptions built into the data are discriminatory. Past data represents past mistakes.

- What ethics and value issues do you identify?
- What would you do?

Scenario: Project partners

Your manager asks you to represent the information service on a prestigious AI project involving a large number of external partners. Feeling rather proud to be chosen, you go to the project kick-off meeting.

The first speaker is the project lead, John, representing a well-known Big Tech company. You have read some rather damning things about his company in the recent news, but actually he gives a rather inspiring speech about the potential of the AI technology to improve lives. Pleasingly he spends a lot of time talking about the protection of privacy, but this seems to be his main ethical focus. This strikes you as rather narrow. You ask about the environmental impact of the computing resource likely to be used by the technology. John seems uneasy with the question and says that this is a technical issue that is well under control.

From the next presentation it appears that one of the companies supplying data to the project is making heavy use of click-workers. You ask about how much these workers are paid. The speaker struggles to answer. He says his expertise is in data integration and he does not really deal with data processing. Most of this is outsourced, he says. He promises to ask colleagues.

Thinking about who is at the meeting, you are also concerned about the representation of user groups. When you raise this, you are told that this is covered in the project plan by focus groups of users of a prototype in month 11 (at the end of the project). A related question you ask is about provision for people with limited digital access or skills: are the benefits of the AI system only for those who are digitally connected? Again, this does not seem to have been thought about.

You are beginning to be quite troubled about a number issues, but you are also aware that you are the only one asking these sort of questions. It strikes you looking around the room nearly everyone is a middle-aged, White male.

In the lunch break you ask John about how responsible operations are being handled in the project. He says his company's ethics team are not represented directly on the project but will carry out a review of the initial design.

He doesn't seem very happy by the line of questioning and you are worried that you are beginning to sound like a technophobe and that your questions might not reflect well on your organisation or the profession.

- What ethics and value issues do you identify?
- What would you do?

Activity 3

Return to your story from the last chapter, where you imagined how AI might better converse with the user. In the light of ethics issues raised in this chapter, how might you further update this conversation, for example:

1 How might the broader concept of socially meaningful transparency reshape how you think about making the working of the AI chatbot better understood?
2 What would a human-centric AI chatbot look like?
3 How could issues of equity be represented?
4 How might AI actively work to help the user manage their privacy, and defuse any sense of surveillance?
5 How would the impact of AI on work be best represented?
6 How can the environmental costs of AI searches be presented to the user?

To think through these issues, redraft an imaginary conversation between your ethical AI chatbot and users.

5

AI and Libraries: An Overview

Introduction

As we have seen in a previous chapter, the discourses around AI makes many promises. These apply in library contexts too. Indeed, there are many ways it seems AI could be used in library services. If we look at the kinds of functions AI performs mentioned in Chapter 2 the relevance is obvious:

- inputting – digitisation of text, manuscripts, images
- transcribing – turning sound recordings and videos into text
- outputting – producing results in different formats
- classifying – creating metadata about content
- summarising – producing abstracts or lay summaries
- recommendation – offering suggestions to users based on previous searches or persistent interests
- translation – translating texts from across languages
- prediction – estimating user behaviour from past patterns
- generation – creation of documents in a particular format.

More concretely, there has been a host of literature weighing up possible uses in library contexts and what might shape which are chosen (e.g. Cox, 2022; Cox and Mazumdar, 2023). At the current time visions linked to generative AI predominate, perhaps in an unfortunate way, as it could be that the unlocking of dark, uncatalogued collections that could be the most useful application in the library context.

One could list possible uses such as in:

1. Digitisation processes. OCR is itself essentially an AI technology. Recent developments such as generative AI support improved recognition, e.g. by enhancing guesses about hard-to-digitise types of content. Advances in voice recognition, handwriting interpretation, etc., also promise to improve the accuracy of digitisation.
2. AI applications to collection description:

   (a) Metadata creation for new content, be that text, manuscripts, images, sound files or moving images. There is a growing literature exploring how AI can contribute to the automatic description of material, both basic bibliographic description and subject description (Lowagie, 2025). Generic AI chatbots have some capabilities, but probably need very careful prompting or bespoke solutions. It is much more likely that AI make suggestions to a human metadata creator than that they take on the whole task.
   (b) Converting between standards of metadata.
   (c) Quality checking across metadata collections, e.g. to identify use of inappropriate language or missing elements.
   (d) Enhancing metadata by adding AI-generated elements.
   (e) Description of collections not previously catalogued manually, 'dark collections'.
   (f) Recommendation systems.
3. User-facing chatbot services that could perform various tasks, from responding to queries to supporting service delivery (this is discussed in much greater depth in Chapter 8).
4. Back-end data manipulation in general. This would be likely to be metadata but it could also be user data.
5. Data services to AI research communities or data scientist communities in the organisation.
6. Analysis of user data to predict patterns in behaviour.
7. Reference enquiry support.
8. Generative AI chatbot use for office tasks (explored more in Chapter 7).
9. AI literacy or competency training for users or staff. While not an application to library services themself, given AI's impact on the information environment in all contexts raising user awareness is a key potential library role (explored in Chapter 6).
10. Other advisory services, such as about the procurement of AI applications.
11. Robots, e.g. for shelf checking, shelf tidying, processing book returns, moving heavy loads of physical books. The current focus in the sector is not robotics, because the centrality of physical book collections has declined. However, it is likely that there might be a return to this focus, especially in the context of automated storage and retrieval systems that support the management of large off-shelf collections.

Thus, there are a wide range of potential applications of AI across library services. Some of these could be potentially transformational, to reflect some of the grander claims about AI. For example, making dark, uncatalogued collections of material much more visible with AI-generated metadata could be transformational for access to such material. Translation seems also very promising to widen access to knowledge. Perhaps insights into user behaviour could be transformational. Some of the other changes might produce greater efficiencies or improved service, without any sort of digital transformation as such.

At the time of writing it seems that the adoption of most of these possibilities remains in their early days, in most library sectors. Our CILIP survey in the UK showed limited use (Cox, 2025a). There is perhaps more development in Asia than in North America and Europe, but most libraries are still exploring options (Clarivate, 2025). Rather the main response to AI has tended to focus on AI literacy training.

In practice libraries seem to focus on raising AI literacy, and direct uses in library services have been generally much slower – with some exceptions. Some of this chapter examines why take-up of AI has been perhaps slower than one might have expected. It also considers how libraries can respond strategically.

The focus on AI literacy is actually quite easy to explain. Firstly, in the educational context where the impact of AI chatbots has created so much concern, there is both a user need and an institutional driver to raise AI literacy. Students at all levels have taken up the easy helpful technologies, with educators struggling to keep up and define learning and assessments that maintain integrity. Institutions recognise that teaching AI literacy is itself an important new part of the curriculum in almost every subject, e.g. for employability. In that context AI literacy training is a pressing user need and institutional driver. More directly, as AI use impacts library collection use, there is a need for libraries to educate users about the information limits of AI chatbots to maintain use of their own material.

Secondly, libraries are the natural place, or one of the natural places, to promote AI literacy, as they already do a lot of information literacy and academic skills training. Indeed, it is fair to say that the profession has a strong educational focus. Thus, teaching AI literacy could be said to align to professional identity.

A third factor is that teaching AI literacy requires less resource than many other responses to AI, such as building or licensing one's own AI systems. In the context of limited resources, focusing on a training role is far less resource-intensive.

Explaining the slow take-up of AI in library services in most sectors

Arguably, then, we could see the take-up of AI in library services, as opposed to AI literacy training, as having progressed rather slowly. For example, it does not seem that very many libraries have developed AI chatbots, even though this has been suggested for at least a decade.

This aligns to studies of other sectors beyond libraries. For example, Google's study with Hypothesis Group published late in 2025 found that most organisations were still at the stage of exploring AI, had gained some time savings but had not been transformed by it (Google Workspace, 2025). They also found employees less optimistic than executives, although other studies suggest a strong demand for AI from frontline staff (IBM, 2025).

If this is a fair characterisation we can seek an explanation for the 'slow' take-up of AI in library services in two types of way. Firstly, it is likely to be something to do with the technology; secondly, to do with libraries' AI capacity or resources.

The nature of the technology makes it hard to manage or govern. Firstly, its development is being shaped outside libraries but is having significant impacts on libraries' core business of providing access to information. Whereas the adoption and implementation of new technology in an organisation is usually a careful process following well understood principles, here adoption has happened outside institutional control, by users. This is perhaps the most novel aspect of AI, though paralleled by the arrival of the web or Google as a search engine. Furthermore, as AI continues to rapidly evolve and change, it is hard to know how to respond, especially as the technologies are presented as having immense potential benefit, yet evidence of applications with a proven return on investment are hard to find, and AI is surrounded by controversy. The benefits in practice are unclear: a 2025 study suggested that 95% of companies are getting zero return from AI. They called this the GenAI divide, because GenAI has been adopted but only increases individual productivity; enterprise-level to transform the organisation have low success (Challapally et al., 2025). In addition, all applications are surrounded by a cloud of controversy. In short, the uncertainty about the direction and benefit around AI as a technology makes it hard for libraries to define a clear response.

The second explanation of slow uptake of AI in library services would be around libraries' capacity to respond. This could be examined through a capability perspective. The concept of AI capability is from the resource-based view of the organisation, and for AI has been developed by Mikalef and Gupta (2021). As with any capability analysis there are some strengths to the approach, such as recognising the uniqueness of each organisation and what resources it has. It also acknowledges the importance of intangible resources. However, the resource-based view is often seen as not giving sufficient weight to the inter-relation of resources. Also, the capability approach tends to ignore factors external to the organisation and take a rather static view of the strengths of the organisation, which is not helpful in highly dynamic contexts. Nevertheless, it can be seen as a useful lens for starting to think about some of the factors shaping the adoption of AI in library services.

AI capability has been defined as consisting of the following elements (Mikalef and Gupta, 2021):

- material resources: data, infrastructure, time and money
- human resources: technical skills and business skills
- intangible resources: ability to co-ordinate a response, ability to change, willingness to take risk.

In our paper Pinar and Cox (2025) we suggested this might need to be extended in the library context to include a depth of AI literacy among all staff under 'human resources' and a capability to understand and manage ethical concerns under 'intangible resources'.

If we take a range of libraries, we would probably consider that there are a number of gaps in library resources against conception of AI capability:

- Data – many libraries have limited data ownership, because typically they license knowledge content. They may have blocks of internal content be that the content of research output repositories or internal research reports. They may have some data about users. But they do not have vast, well organised collections of data that they own.
- Resources – many libraries, especially in the public sector, are already over-stretched.
- Infrastructure – for many libraries this may be out of date and controlled by others.
- Technical skills – many libraries buy in technologies like library systems and content systems, rather than develop their own. They have limited capability to develop AI solutions, even where open-source solutions exist.
- Management skills – libraries have a good history of responding to new technologies and implementing solutions. So, these skills are more likely to be present.
- Staff AI literacy – there is some fear and hesitation around the technology, as well as justified ethical concerns, blocking development of AI skills.

- Co-ordination – libraries may be good at co-ordinating internally but often exist in complex wider institutions.
- Change capacity – public sector may be quite weak in its ability to change rapidly.
- Risk taking – again, the public sector may be quite poor at managing risk.
- Ethics capability – libraries may be quite well equipped in this area.

Differences in need and capability

While the analysis above suggests that for many libraries there are significant gaps in capability, it is evident that the multiple nature of AI impacts different library sectors differently, because they have different needs and capabilities. This may qualify our picture of slow take-up of AI in library services.

National libraries in some countries in North America, Western Europe and Australia and New Zealand, and some rich research libraries in those same regions, stand out as an exception to the pattern of slow take-up of AI. The AI4LAM community has operated as a vibrant community for such institutions and in their exciting Fantastic Futures conferences AI4LAM have been at the forefront of demonstrating the possibilities of AI technologies, from well before the emergence of generative AI (AI4LAM, 2026).

The dynamism of this sector is driven by two sources of need:

1. Through their legal deposit role, they acquire huge amounts of print and born-digital material every year. They have needed AI to seek to manage the scale of these acquisitions.
2. Through their projects to digitise their unique and culturally significant historical collections for scholarship and the public. Again, the scale of the need is huge; the need to digitise the content effectively and to create metadata to manage collections and allow users to navigate the content means that AI offers attractive solutions. AI is helpful here especially in digitising diverse types of content such as manuscripts, audio and video.

Relatively well resourced institutions in these roles have the need and a greater capability to develop AI solutions than most libraries. They have the data and some of the technical development expertise to develop AI solutions. This is in contrast to the average academic library, which would be more likely to be licensing solutions from publishers and other intermediaries. Equally, many national libraries and archives that are less well resourced, such as in smaller regional institutions, and those outside the most prosperous parts of the world would lack the necessary resources.

Even such well resourced institutions face challenges such as (Mergel and Schmidt, 2025):

- the sheer scale of content they are trying to handle;
- lack of clarity over the copyright status of content;
- limited financial and technical resources, compared to the scale of the need and opportunities. Moving from projects to full services is seen to be challenging.
- gaps in staff skills across the organisation;
- the challenges created by trying to work with other institutions such as tech companies or even researchers with their different motives;
- accuracy of AI outputs, especially trying to use AI trained on modern content on historic data. A particularly important aspect of this is the dominance of the English language in AI development. National libraries in the non-English speaking parts of the world have an important role in preserving the cultural vitality of other languages. They can play a leading role in wider initiatives to stimulate AI development. Their collections in non-English language are an invaluable training resource. It is worrying, however, that resource restraints in many national contexts, particularly in the Global South, mean that AI driven by Big Tech does pose a threat to linguistic diversity.
- creating explainable AI;
- lack of clarity about the ethics of using AI.

These are similar to the challenges that smaller libraries and archives with unique collections face. In this sense what the AI4LAM community is developing may be a place where the whole library world learns about AI.

For example, Lee's (2023) synthesis of checklists and guidance on the use of AI for machine learning with heritage collections already brings together much of the wisdom learned over many years around ethical considerations in 'collections as data' for AI uses, especially in the light of a growing concern to decolonise collections. This prompts institutions to think about such issues as:

1 What is the provenance of the collection? Many historic collections were collected in ways that might now be deemed inappropriate.
2 What individuals and communities are represented in any collection, considering their right to a say in their own representation? For example, indigenous communities have rights over their own data.
3 What other groups and communities, including target users, might be involved, and how can they be informed about the meaning of the use of machine learning and its limits if any? How will use be evaluated?

4 If the collection has already been digitised, how was the choice made to prioritise it for digitisation and how complete was that process? We know historic decision making about digitisation often reflected cultural biases.
5 What is the copyright status of the collection?
6 If crowd labour was involved in such processes as digitisation, was this ethically conducted, e.g. were rewards and recognition appropriate?
7 How is the model used to apply to the collection evaluated, e.g. in terms of potential for accuracy, bias or environmental impact?
8 How will documentation and training data be shared with other projects?

Some of these broad considerations are relevant to other contexts, for example by extension the same questions can be asked about any collection that is licensed. However, the position for most academic libraries or most public libraries in relation to AI would be rather different. Here the issue is much more about AI literacy and possibly making choices about licensing AI systems.

The position for a small school library is hardly comparable at all. Here uptake of AI chatbots may have been particularly rapid (by students and staff) while staff resources could be very limited.

In other sectors different dynamics are at work, e.g. in the corporate or legal sector there could be a greater focus on business intelligence applications of AI, using AI to make internal documentation more available while protecting confidentiality.

The wider context within which AI is landing

A further reflection relating to how libraries respond to AI may be to consider the wider context within which it is landing, both the existing local organisational structures and traditions, but also the other aspects of the external environment. These aspects are downplayed by the capability model, so it is useful to remind ourselves of what they are. By definition, it is not possible to fully describe these, but likely aspects might be:

- Strategic emphasis being placed by government on AI. The OECD AI policy observatory (https://oecd.ai/en) reveals that many countries around the world have their own AI strategy. If we take the UK as an example, it has had several national strategies, but there are also strategies at sector level, such as for the UK National Health Service. There is also a research funder policy on AI. National and sector level policies set the context within which libraries operate. While a strategic priority, the development of AI regulation seems much more tenuous.

- Economic struggles. At the time of writing in early 2026 there appears to continue to be widespread economic slowdown, meaning that libraries across sectors and their institutions are struggling with funding in every area of activity. This can reduce resources for proof-of-concept projects, lead to the loss of skilled staff, and proscribe opportunities for staff development. It may put pressure on institutions to use AI to cut costs.
- The risk environment. Widespread uncertainty arguably reduces the willingness to take risk. This may underlie a depth of caution in responding to AI.
- Polycrisis. As the most important challenge of the times, it is hard to underestimate the importance of the climate crisis. We have discussed this extensively in Chapter 4. Some have talked about us living in an age of polycrisis, with very heightened levels of uncertainty. The sense of information crisis discussed in Chapter 3 may be an aspect of this.

Tactics to raise library AI capability

In a context of AI as a complex, rapidly changing technology with multiple potential uses across the library – in such a context of uncertainty – it seems there are a number of possible ways to increase capability, but no simple path forwards (Cox, 2024b). The levels of uncertainty with AI make it hard to be sure what is the best approach. If very clear use cases emerged then there would be an ability to invest in that direction; in the absence of this, library strategy is likely to be more broad-brush stroke.

A Google Workspace study (2025) suggested that organisations that had been transformed by AI: (1) had a clear strategy and roadmap; (2) integrated AI into company culture; (3) prioritised AI across tasks; (4) empowered AI advocacy across the organisation; and (5) sustained investment in tools and training. However, in a context of uncertainty it is quite unclear how libraries might make these changes.

Libraries respond by adopting some or many of the potential tactics described below, and they could be organised into a planned roadmap. The interventions can be interlinked, but for clarity we can divide the potential tactics into five types: informational, organisational, workforce developmental, relational and project-related.

Informational tactics

Logically the first focus might be informational, seeking to lower uncertainty around the technology. So, environment scanning would look at:

- wider trends around AI, such as strategies of the Big Tech companies
- sector trends, e.g. in edtech for libraries operating in that sector
- library technology supplier trends
- trends in technologies for a selected task such as administration or research support
- trends in library practice, especially searching for best practices in AI use in the same library sector, including shared resources such as open educational resources.

More internally focused information gathering could look at studying how user behaviour is changing or studying library staff attitudes:

- changes in user behaviour and attitudes, through analysis of database use statistics, surveying, interviews and focus groups
- library staff uses of generative AI and attitudes.

Organisational tactics

Here the focus is on creating new organisational arrangements that co-ordinate or underpin a response to AI and the change management required:

- Appointment of a senior or expert member of staff to co-ordinate responses to AI across the organisation.
- Policy. The very process of trying to develop a policy might be beneficial in bringing different viewpoints together. A policy would help build trust in uses by the library. Policies could be of different sorts. A policy could define the broad stance towards AI, define how AI should or should not be used, or even lay out an explicit framework for how AI technologies will be evaluated. A high-level policy is likely to relate strongly to what we have discussed in the AI ethics chapter. It will explain its relation to other policies and strategies. However, the more definitive such statements are the more they are likely to need changing.
- A working group or task-and-finish group with a specific remit to deliver on a particular task relating to AI, such as developing a policy or running a project. The question becomes what the terms of reference for such a group might be.
- An evolving communications plan – communicating the library's approach will be a key task for the working group.
- A community of practice – a similar approach but seeking to create a more informal knowledge-sharing community. In the context of uncertainty this might be a more plausible approach than a goal-directed working group. The community is likely to be in the form of talks from the community sharing experiences, including failures. It is

a gradual and bottom-up way to build trust and relationships. It is a foundation for a more coherent institutional approach.

Workforce development tactics

Staff may need new skills and perhaps a shift of attitudes. So a workforce development tactic is as much about change management as purely about upskilling. However, in a context of uncertainty, it is a little hard to say what knowledge, skills and attitudes are needed, and by whom. Presumably some staff need more technical appreciation, while others might just need a general awareness (as convincingly defined by the ACRL (2025) framework discussed in Chapter 6). There are a number of potential tactics here:

- recruitment of expert staff. but this is not very realistic given the high demand for AI expertise
- upskilling existing staff, by
  - staff training, such as through a bespoke course or jointly taking an external course, with local discussion
  - reading groups
  - attendance at professional events
  - encouraging staff to take work time to experiment with AI and share learning with team members
  - building skill development into appraisal criteria
  - active involvement in a library project to employ AI
  - internal conferences.

Relational tactics

This is about aligning to the institutional direction of travel and building up the new relationships and collaborations needed to respond to AI, since like other major changes it is unlikely to be a task that needs to be achieved by the library alone. Working collaboratively broadens resources, increases trust and reduces risk. In the first instance relational tactics must ensure that the library aligns to developments in their wider institution, or potentially takes a lead in shaping organisational strategy in some areas.

In terms of more horizontal collaborations, these could be built on existing collaborations but also could be new ones. Working with other groups effectively increases the available resources and skills. It may also be important to maintaining trust in the library brand. In the first instance mapping internal and external relationships relevant to AI would be a useful task. For example, in a university context likely partners are:

- IT
- other professional services, such as those that support staff development
- academic departments
- research centres with an AI focus
- user groups
- other stakeholders.

There are highly likely to be cross-organisational working groups that the library would seek to contribute to. In addition, there are external actors with whom the library could work: such as system suppliers wishing to have development partners, other libraries, or even AI developers. Creating an expert panel to guide the library development could be a useful initiative.

Proof-of-concept and flagship projects

One way to focus effort might be to develop a proof-of-concept or even a flagship AI project. This would work with other tactics to focus organisational attention, instantiate policy, help develop skills and understand how to integrate AI into existing workflows. Possible projects could include:

- an exhibition about AI, simply based on items in the collection about AI, given how topical it is
- an AI project focused on library content, such as to enhance metadata about a collection, e.g. dissertations
- audit local data resources to identify issues of data quality and ownership
- create some applications using local data
- get involved in a project in the wider institution.

A roadmap

It is likely that a set of tactics would be used to increase capability. These could be planned as a roadmap. For example, the following is a plausible mapping:

Phase 1

- staff encouraged to explore using AI in their own work
- exploration of how AI is changing information behaviours of users through a survey
- horizon scanning of technology, in sector, and within institution
- appoint senior lead to co-ordinate AI response.

Phase 2
- staff development community of practice
- proof-of-concept project
- developing web guides and advice
- search for collaborators inside the institution
- policy work, including defining requirements for suppliers.

Phase 3
- recruit developer staff
- major project to develop AI based services.

Visions of AI and the library

To a large extent the development of AI may lie outside the control of the library and the library's response must be allowed to emerge. Yet in developing AI capabilities it would be productive to have a vision in mind of how the library will use AI. It may be possible to articulate some potential visions of what AI can achieve in the library context:

- The automated library. AI is primarily seen as for background processing of data.
- The responsive library. AI is primarily seen as a means to provide 24/7 service.
- The living systematic review. AI automates part or whole of the literature review process, allowing researchers to stay current despite the scale and publication rate around a topic.
- The AI learning space. The library as a hub of learning and experiment about AI, perhaps inspired by maker space ideas.
- The intelligent library. AI offers wholly new ways to interact with the content collection, such as by navigating across the full text of its entire content.
- The public or community AI. Where the library actively participates in the creation of non-commercial, publicly beneficial AI.

Conclusion

Libraries can potentially benefit from AI in many ways, though we seem to be in early days in most libraries in most sectors. There is a current focus on AI literacy.

We are beginning to see case studies of real uses of AI more widely than just in the most well-resourced libraries. A report for Clarivate (Emerging strategy, 2026) made the case for how the use of AI in metadata creation and reading list handling increases efficiency, speeds up processing, and shifts staffing to more oversight roles.

Of course, such shifts in productivity are likely to also impact employment levels.

Libraries can be important players in constructing a discourse of responsible AI. By developing ethical AI in their own operations and contributing to wider AI understanding they are helping to create a socially more responsible approach to AI. National libraries can play a particularly critical role, because they are developing AI applications and their unique resources can contribute to public or community AI (Public AI Network, 2025). Asking questions like the ones posed in the IFLA Entry Point change the discussion around AI, challenging suppliers to be more ethical in how they implement AI.

Activity

Shaping library strategy: a role-play narrative

The University of Poppleton library team are meeting to discuss the potential to create an AI policy for the library. They are considering a number of options, such as a high-level statement of principle or perhaps a much more specific set of requirements to be applied to evaluating AI applications.

While AI is being debated, persistent drivers of institutional strategy remain important: such as the need for a reputation for excellent research, high-quality student experiences and employability, a strong relation with local communities. Will how the library contributes through its staff, services, spaces and collections be reshaped by AI?

Some of the main protagonists in the debate are listed below with a short description of their stance.

- The library director. They have two main thoughts on AI. Firstly, they are concerned about how the library sits in the institution and the need to align or even show leadership in the context of AI, to protect library resourcing. Realistically they feel the current circumstances are pointing to increasing pressure on budgets. There may need to be a downscaling of subscriptions and even some shifts in staff roles. They realise AI might contribute to savings but are worried about staff responses to change. They want hard evidence about the benefit of AI before they make a commitment. Equally, the institution recognises the need to raise student and staff AI literacy and is investing in it. Showing the library's role in delivering on the institution's promises on AI is essential. The second perspective the library director brings to the debate is the need to think long-term about the big long-term environmental trends that could impact the library. They are in close contact with similar institutions, trying to understand how they are responding to new challenges. This chapter has discussed some of those considerations.

- The user services lead feels there are more important priorities for student experience, such as provision of high-quality learning materials, comfortable learning spaces in the library building, and proactive well-being support. They have looked at AI chatbot services but consider the human touch essential to what users value, so do not think it is a good use of resources to invest in AI compared to the existing human-based chat service.
- The learning and teaching lead is focused on further developing useful resources for students and staff to understand ethical use of AI in the teaching context. They have already introduced a big strand of AI awareness training in their academic skills offering. But it is difficult to adapt this fully across the many disciplines being taught. They desperately need more resources to develop this material. They are also very aware of some faculty concerns about the impact on learning and entrenched resistance to any use of AI. They are not quite sure how to proceed with upskilling academic staff, which falls more in the remit of other services. There are already good relationships with other professional services teams such as co-ordination with staff development, student support, disability support and the careers service. They are interested in a project to examine employability.
- The scholarly communications lead feels that AI is an important topic with some strong positives but a high degree of risk surrounding it. There are some glowing examples of how scholars in the university are using AI that should be showcased, including by some digital humanists, though they are not using local library collections. At the same time, there is a need to respect disciplinary differences in research practices. There is an institutional reputational risk around misuse, especially through the proliferation of AI tools for literature reviewing or even data analysis. There is some troubling evidence about how doctoral students are using AI. They feel there is a need for some sort of review of how researchers are using AI.
- The IT lead is dismissive of generative AI as rather trivial and inaccurate, but they see huge potential in other forms of AI to save time and increase accuracy in the manipulation of backend data in the library management system. From their technically informed perspective they view others as confused about the real issues around

AI. They are also frustrated by slow release of AI functionality by the current system supplier.
- The special collection lead is keen to find partners for a project to digitise the library's unique collection of autobiographies. They have found enthusiasm from a couple of academic departments and are hoping to gain the library director's support to invest time in developing a proposal for external funding.
- The strategy committee includes a young professional in an attempt to diversify perspectives. They are themselves an enthusiast for AI, partly because they are studying a part-time Master's and their dissertation is about the topic. However, they are highly concerned that many library staff are resistant to experimenting with AI and have an unspoken worry about the implications for their jobs. The young professional would like to see a wider debate about the ethics of AI across the library staff, especially in areas such as the environmental impact of AI.

How to use this scenario:

- If you are operating in a different type of context parts of the scenario may need to be adjusted.
- Update the profiles as you think relevant to your context.

If it is a group exercise, individuals or teams can be given one of the roles to further develop and play out that have been defined above.

The role play could be around:

- The initial discussions about the library stance towards AI
- A follow-up, a year on. The kind of things that might have changed could be:
  - Institutional policy about the use of AI in learning or research has been more tightly defined through a traffic-light system defined at module level.
  - Gathering evidence of decline in library collection use.
- There is an opportunity to participate in a trial of AI-based updates to the library management system, do the different protagonists think this is something the library should prioritise?

6

AI Competencies

Introduction

A recurrent feature of national AI strategies around the world is recognition of an AI skills gap (Papyshev and Yarime, 2023). This may often focus on high-level computational and data science skills in the IT workforce to develop or implement AI. However, the pervasive use of AI and rapid take-up of generative AI implies a need for a much wider level of understanding of the subject in society. AI seems to be increasingly relevant to every worker in all industries, since it seems to have implications across so many. Also, it is relevant to every citizen, because of everyday uses of AI to access information and for other purposes, because of the implications of the use of AI by government services, and because of its impact on access to information within democratic processes. To state the obvious, this is not about everyone having technical skills to develop AI, but rather a widespread understanding of its use and social implications. The question becomes 'Who should know what: and what would constitute AI literacy or competence?'

This chapter explores the nature of AI competencies, primarily from an LIS perspective. In LIS we have a tradition of talking about skills as literacies. The terms skills may be more widely understood. Competencies is probably the best term, because it includes attitudes as well as knowledge and skills.

AI competencies are hard to define because:

- AI is inherently hard to understand, as it is based on advanced computation and statistics.
- Of course, it is fair to acknowledge that most of us do not understand many aspects of everyday life that we depend on. Many drivers would struggle to explain how a car engine works. We can drive a car safely if we understand how to operate the controls and the rules of the road. We do not necessarily need to know what is going on beneath the hood. So, it remains to reflect on what do particular groups in society need to know? Different groups need different types of knowledge: therefore it may not be possible to give a general definition.

- AI seems to be changing fast and is likely to evolve rapidly in the coming years. It is proliferating across platforms and tending to disappear into the infrastructure, into the background – so it is hard for the user to know when it is even operating.
- Big Tech does not want AI to be transparent, e.g. they have been secretive about training data and environmental impact and even when it's in use. The way AI chatbots present themselves adds to AI's opacity.

Despite these difficulties one could argue that the need for AI competencies is already a failure: arguably, AI should be transparent and explainable to all users, so that a minimum literacy would be required. This probably could be achieved by developers if they took the time and resource to design AI transparently as well as following the precepts of socially meaningful transparency, as discussed in Chapter 4. However, given that there is little sign of this happening there is a need for AI competencies.

It is easy to get excited about a role in promoting AI competencies. However, I believe that the debate should be as much about the potential loss of skills that are replaced or devalued by AI, not just on new skills. If AI through its functions of summarisation is reducing our reading skills and, by accelerating demands, is blocking slower, more considered forms of thinking we should think of AI as a deskilling process as much as an upskilling event.

The overall impact of AI on learning and skills is contested. AI has the potential to offer adaptive and interactive learning experiences. It may be beneficial for those with learning disabilities. The wonder around AI makes learning exciting. Equally there have been questions about its impact on critical thinking, on the social dimension of learning, on our creativity and ability to develop our own voice in writing (Crawford et al., 2024; Habib et al., 2024; Cardon et al., 2023).

At some level, there should be a right to refuse AI. If one examines it and finds it a barrier to good learning, or unhelpful or damaging for society, there must be room for a refusal to use it.

What we have presented in Chapter 3 shows that LIS has a key role here, because it has a relevant perspective (and critique) of AI. However, there is probably always a need to work with other groups to round out a conception of AI competency.

Some would prefer simply to reiterate existing information literacy advice, since general principles of critical evaluation of information apply as much to AI-generated contexts as any other. AI training should be embedded within wider information literacy and information skills. For others it is a new area of practice.

Many definitions of AI competencies

Many definitions of AI skills have appeared in the last couple of years (like the many AI principles that have been published). Often these include skills relating to the creation of AI – not so relevant for us in the library context. Most of the definitions of AI competency presented in the chapter are explicitly in resistance to purely technical definitions for computer scientists as those building AI systems and barely mention ethical issues.

Another well established strand of thought that should not be forgotten is all the work around a definition of algorithmic literacy. This was developed in the context of interacting with platforms where experiences are being shaped by filtering and recommending systems. A good definition is from Dogruel, Masur and Joeckel (2022):

> Algorithm literacy can thus be defined as being aware of the use of algorithms in online applications, platforms, and services, knowing how algorithms work, being able to critically evaluate algorithmic decision-making as well as having the skills to cope with or even influence algorithmic operations.

Generative AI literacy model

I will take as a starting point the model we ourselves developed in one project (Zhao, Cox and Cai, 2024; Cox, 2024a).

1. Pragmatic understanding: the individual can use generative AI effectively and interpret the information it produces critically. We break this ability down into three aspects:
   (a) The individual can pick the right tool for the task, in the context of the proliferation of platforms (including alternative generative AI to ChatGPT).
   (b) The individual learns to use the chosen tool effectively for a specific task. To a large extent this boils down to writing better prompts: 'prompt engineering'.
   (c) The individual interprets generative AI outputs critically, given an understanding of how they work and their limits. The user needs to think about issues like accuracy and bias.
2. Safety understanding: the individual can use generative AI while protecting their own privacy and the confidentiality of others.
3. Reflective understanding: the individual can assess and take action to manage the impacts of AI on their experience. This relates to the need to make conscious decisions about when and how to use AI, given how such use might impact their own skills or learning.

4 Socio-ethical understanding: the individual must have a rounded appreciation of the societal impacts of AI, including IPR issues, impacts on information culture, social impacts, environmental impacts and the undue power of Big Tech. We have discussed these issues extensively in previous chapters.
5 Contextual understanding: the individual understands how to use generative AI appropriately in a particular context and make their own use explicit, as appropriate. Thus, for example, using it for wording some informal correspondence or making personal plans is a very different context from its use for an assessed task in education or in a critical or confidential workplace task.

Our definition is explicitly about generative AI not AI in general.

It would be fair to say our definition focuses on information finding and use, especially in an educational context, reflecting that it was developed out of a study of student use of generative AI. It does not say anything about recognising when AI has been used, which could also be deemed a form of AI literacy, one already discussed in the concept of algorithmic literacy.

This model does not say much about understanding underlying AI technologies or familiarity with the meaning of terms such as machine learning or neural nets. I have always been doubtful of building AI literacy for most people by explaining such technical concepts, especially as this is often suggested as a foundational start. Few people understand the explanation and it is not really clear how it progresses actual practical use or social implications. I certainly think it is important to establish that current AI is based on statistical predictions of probability derived from 'data' it has been trained on, with the implications that it can predict wrongly, especially if the data is biased or inaccurate. Plus, the idea of an algorithm that is chosen for the task and tweaked to get the best percentage results helps us understand that most AI answers are predictions with a more or less acceptable degree of accuracy. There is quite a good statement of this in the AILit framework (discussed below) under the heading 'the nature of AI'.

Educause Framework for AI literacy (Hibbert et al., 2024)

One of the strengths of this model is its simplicity and clarity. It has four basic elements:

1 understand AI – understand terminology and key concepts
2 use and apply AI – prompting and effective use
3 analyse and evaluate AI – reflect critically on outputs and awareness of wider ethical issues

4 create AI – build AI systems.

Although billed as an AI literacy model, it is quite oriented towards generative AI, e.g. in its stress on prompting in the second section.

UNESCO's AI competency framework

UNESCO's (2024) AI competency framework is a much more complex model, and as one would expect shows a more global, ethically driven perspective. Its core principles are fivefold.

Firstly, being critical. It is widely agreed that taking a critical stance towards AI is important, but it is not always clear what this term means. UNESCO explain that AI competency should:

> . . . prepare students with the values, knowledge and skills necessary to critically examine the proportionality of AI from an ethical perspective. This includes examining and understanding its impact on human agency, social inclusion and equity, institutional and individual security, cultural and linguistic diversity, the construction and expression of plural opinions, as well as on the environment and on ecosystems.
>
> (UNESCO, 2024)

We can largely agree with this very broad perspective on the social risks of AI, often neglected by AI statements. For example, the AILit framework reviewed in the next section tends to imply being critical is to be equated simply with 'critical thinking' about AI outputs. At the same time it feels like there is a lack of a socio-technical appreciation of the power of Big Tech or the geopolitics around AI even in the UNESCO approach.

The second principle of UNESCO's model is to affirm the need for a 'human-centric' approach. It is a recurring theme to think about human agency and values in the context of AI. We quoted UNESCO's scoping of this idea in Chapter 4.

This both works at an abstract level to retain a concern with human dignity and agency, and more practically implies other principles such as explainability.

The third UNESCO competency principle is to assert the centrality of environmental sustainability. Again, this is a good correction to more pragmatic models, like the previous ones discussed, which may mention the environment but place it less centrally. Of course, one could say that a planetary-centric AI might be in tension with the idea of a human-centric AI.

Inclusivity is the fourth UNESCO principle. What they mean here is that students should learn inclusive design principles: 'This covers the selection of representative data, the choice of bias-agnostic algorithms and anti-discrimination training methods, the design of accessible functionalities, testing for the inclusiveness of AI outputs, and impact assessment of the use of AI on social inclusion.'

The fifth principle is the need for a lifelong approach, given the long-term impact of AI and its changing nature. This argues for a focus on underlying principles, unlike the focus on generative AI literacy in our own model.

The competency framework itself has four competency aspects (Human-centred mindset, Ethics of AI, AI techniques and applications and AI system design) and three progression levels (understand, apply, create). While wordy and rather complex, the UNESCO approach is likely to be a key reference point going forward in the context of proliferating AI competency models.

AILit framework (OECD, 2025)

At the time of writing the AILit framework from European Commission and OECD is still under review, but it is useful to review some of its founding principles:

- Interdisciplinary nature of AI literacy. Although as it happens the list of subjects included does not include LIS, it is useful to draw attention to the need for many perspectives on AI to be brought together.
- Foundational.
- Illustrative – scenarios are not yet developed in any depth, but this feels useful in moving beyond generalised statements of skills that are hard to operationalise.
- Global – world wide applicability.
- Practical.
- Durable – a key point as AI evolves.

There are some strong elements to the model. It is easy to understand and engagingly illustrated. It is much more accessible than the UNESCO document. It attempts to bridge the gap to delivery of AI skills by making suggestions of scenarios that could be useful to explain the concept in a primary or secondary school context. It usefully differentiates between engaging with AI, creating with AI and designing and managing AI. As a competency model it articulates some attitudes that it suggests are needed to respond to AI:

- responsible – is linked to accountability in the use of AI
- curious – willingness to explore
- innovative – applies AI to real world challenges

- adaptable – perseverance and flexibility to use AI
- empathetic – reflects about wider impacts of AI on other individuals, communities and society.

ACRL AI competencies for academic library workers

At the time of writing the ACRL (2025) model of AI competences seems the most relevant available, so I am presenting an outline of it in full below:

Mindsets: Curiosity, Scepticism, Judgement, Responsibility and Collaboration

1 Ethical considerations
   - Facilitate and advocate for more equitable access to AI technologies and AI literacy
   - Promote fairness in the use of data and design of AI systems
   - Protect individual autonomy and privacy rights, cultural diversity, and intellectual property rights when using AI systems
   - Ensure appropriate accountability for the design and use of AI systems, including transparency, explainability, accuracy and reliability
   - Consider the broader impacts of AI on communities, workers and the environment.
2 Knowledge and understanding
   - Basic understanding of technologies
   - Understand AI attribution and detection
   - Stay current with AI applications by following reliable sources from a diverse range of experts
   - Critically evaluate sources of information about AI for accuracy and bias
   - Understand AI policies and regulations relevant to your context.
3 Analysis and evaluation
   - Explain AI technologies and their impacts on library services and resources
   - Evaluate the benefits and risks in the deployment of AI technologies
   - Critically analyse AI technologies using a multifaceted approach
   - Evaluate AI tools in the context of library specific tasks and services.
4 Use and application
   - Apply AI for task efficiency and quality enhancement
   - Use AI to facilitate communication and collaboration in the workplace
   - Develop effective prompting strategies for optimal AI output

- Explore the AI capabilities for evaluation
- Select AI tools that are designed for accessibility and usability.

Although it is specifically for the academic sector and originating in a particular country, the ACRL statement will be influential as a clear articulation of what librarians themselves need to know, backed by a respected organisation in the LIS world. It does not differentiate by library role, but this would be nearly impossible given the variation, so we can see it as a statement of what the baseline should be for most professional staff. When there is a clearer picture of AI applications to library work that have a return on investment, the skills for critical roles will emerge.

A real strength is the inclusion of mindsets, and the ones described feel like they fit the case well. The first three mindsets are an articulation of a critical perspective: where opportunities are explored, sceptically evaluated, with an intention to come to a judgement about use. There is a strong sense of agency here. Although the right to refuse AI is not acknowledged, it is explained that AI adoption makes it inevitable that librarians have some understanding of it. Scepticism surely needs to encompass socio-technical understanding of AI as a global industry and focus of geopolitical struggle. The development of this dimension is perhaps a bit lacking. But it is also good that a mindset of responsibility and ethical considerations (section 1) is given priority in the model. The fifth mindset points to the need to collaborate with others. I suppose the one thing that might be thought to be lacking is a reference to the human-centric approach emphasised by UNESCO and also present in the ACRL principles statement. It is interesting that equity of access is given prominence under ethical considerations. Though highly desirable, I wonder how far that is possible in the academic context where inequalities between institutions are deep-rooted.

The knowledge base that is described after this is well articulated. In particular the statements under basic understanding are well chosen. It seems these will need updating rather quickly, but how the level of understanding is pitched seems correct. While sections 2, 3 and 4 seem a little poorly differentiated, they feel like a convincing set of knowledge taken together. The naming of the high-level sections appears to reference the Educause framework. On the whole, the wording of the model applies to AI in general, though the reference specifically to prompt skills in section 4 seems generative AI-specific. One can understand the desire to create a durable model by abstracting principles beyond the current dominant model of AI, but the strength of acknowledging the specifics of generative AI remain.

AI skill development feels like a priority for information professionals. But it's worth acknowledging several important points that offer a context for the ACRL listing. Firstly, we are familiar with the need to update our skills. Things have scarcely stood still in the last decades and librarians are good at learning and updating their skills. Secondly, while some aspects of AI are very new, we have been dealing with AI in some forms for many years, such as AI in search and recommendation. A lot of that understanding remains relevant to generative AI. Thirdly, while the demand for AI skills is growing, this is both technical skills and more general AI literacies. These also sit alongside other skills that are needed to reap its benefits. For example, LinkedIn (2025) finds that AI skill growth is complemented by growth in demand for digital skills, business skills and soft skills. Librarians are strong in these areas: it is a digital skills profession. Fourthly, the core skills employers want include technology skills but remain human-focused. The World Economic Forum (WEF, 2025) finds the following key skills wanted by employers:

1. analytic thinking
2. resilience, flexibility and agility
3. leadership and social influence
4. creative thinking
5. motivation and self-awareness
6. technological literacy
7. empathy and active listening
8. curiosity and lifelong learning
9. talent management
10. service orientation and customer service.

> This combination of cognitive, self-efficacy and interpersonal skills within the top five emphasises the importance ascribed by respondents to having an agile, innovative and collaborative workforce, where both problem-solving abilities and personal resilience are critical for success.
>
> (WEF, 2025, 35)

AI literacy may be growing in importance, but there is a persistence in key attributes of attitudes and human-oriented skills needed across workforces. Finally, while librarians may need to update their skills, so many other professions are experiencing this pressure too, and librarians play key roles in supporting the learning of others.

Developing AI literacy with people who have low or no digital skills

It seems that many of the AI competency models are aimed at the educational sector. Yet AI literacy needs to be for all workers and citizens. Indeed, in the context of existing digital divides the need to be inclusive is vital. For this reason, it is useful to examine the AI literacy principles proposed by the digital inclusion charity, the Good Things Foundation. Their core principles, though high-level, are convincing:

- AI literacy support needs to be centred around practical tasks and tailored to an individual's needs and interests
- Both positives and negatives should be communicated
- AI should be embedded as part of a wider digital skills journey
- Support should be interactive
- Support should be inclusive and flexible

(Good Things Foundation, 2024)

AI competencies need to be embedded in practical tasks of interest to target groups, which are likely to be different from the contexts of interest to young people. AI training could be organised around completing a task of value to the participants.

AI competencies also need to be embedded alongside other skills as part of digital literacy, as well as other interventions. Indeed, we can see AI literacy as needing foundations in digital skills and media skills. There has to be sustained engagement. This helps us understand better the implications of the UNESCO emphasis on inclusivity.

Conclusion

We should not need AI literacy, because either by design or regulation AI should be made meaningfully transparent, both in the sense of being understandable at the point of use but also in the broader social implications of any application. But the reality is that nearly everyone as worker and citizen needs some level of AI competencies.

As well as thinking about new competencies, we need to promote reflection on the potential damage done to existing skills that AI is superseding, undermining or devaluing. It is easy to focus on the positive task of raising AI competencies without recognising that it is in some ways a deskilling technology.

AI competency cannot be equated with technical skills for computer scientists building systems or even 'prompt engineering' as a way of using the particular generative AI technologies effectively. The approach needs to be at an appropriate technical level for different groups of students and other members of society.

It also has to be inclusive in a broad way of the ethics of AI, considering its widest social and international implications, especially environmental sustainability. Indeed, the stress on a 'human-centric' approach asserted in some frameworks could be balanced by a 'planet-centric' approach.

AI literacy should include a right to refuse, in some circumstance or even completely (Sano-Franchini, McIntyre and Fernandes, 2025; Tudorie, 2023). Some of the terminology in AI literacy models, such as the need to be innovative or adaptable, convey a subtle sense that AI use is inevitable. It is easy to characterise refusal as technophobia or fear-driven, and it often is so described (Tudorie, 2023). We should avoid this assumption and make reasonable arrangements to allow people to refuse AI, such as by opt-outs.

It tends to be agreed that AI competency needs to be critical and ethically aware. But we need to be clear about the scope of criticality. As we have seen in Chapter 4, the ethical issues are far from simple, so how to raise understanding here is complex.

Socio-technical understanding highlights the political economy and geopolitical aspects of the AI industry. But AI is also being used and potentially useful – so prompt skills, skills to evaluate outputs are a core part of current AI literacy. The term competencies brings attitudes and mindsets into the equation, so it is not just about knowledge and skills. We have reviewed some relevant terms. AI competencies need to offer an understanding of fundamentals which are durable over time, because the technologies shift rather rapidly and are already widely spread.

At the same time, as the technology evolves there is a need to update our understanding of how AI reshapes the system of information production and distribution as the foundation for AI literacy. Both librarians and users have to be prepared for refreshing their understanding of how information is produced to be a lifelong task.

The sense from the concept of algorithmic literacy that there is often an issue of even being aware that AI is in use needs to be retained, as AI functions appear everywhere and often rather in the background.

The LIS perspective is important to AI literacy, with its stress on the accuracy of outputs, but needs to sit alongside other perspectives, such as from computing, data science, and also philosophy. We need to speak up about the information issues in the context of an interdisciplinary debate but accept the strength of the benefits and learn about its use ourselves.

A wide range of communities need support, not just those now in education. We need to talk to people in language they understand, related to their experiences and needs, and in the context of their need for digital skills as a whole. What AI means needs to be understood contextually but also a model needs to have global applicability.

Most of the models are abstract. Precisely what people should know and the scenarios that are effective in illustrating AI issues will need a lot of thought in context.

Activity

For this chapter I am suggesting that the reader plan out their own scenario, as a story to be used for discussion in an AI training course to generate debate about how to use an AI chatbot effectively. Referring to our model of generative AI literacy can be helpful for thinking about what elements should be included.

Following the guides suggested by Bradshaw (2012) in Chapter 1 is useful:

- Keep the story short – this gives all participants time to read the scenario individually, even in a short session.
- Ensure that the scenario is open-ended – there may well not be a 'correct' answer; rather, embed within the story a number of elements.
- Include relatable detail – set the story in a familiar context that the reader feels is relevant.
- Use humour – having a light-hearted element makes the story more engaging. Avoid stereotyping.

You may want to include prompts for participants or for yourself as part of your scenario composition. We have several examples in the book you can re-read for inspiration. Examples of interesting contexts for a story about using an AI chatbot might be:

1. Writing a job application – raises questions about privacy of personal details, but also effectiveness of AI for writing. What prompts might increase control and distinctiveness of output?
2. Writing an internal report based on analysing user data – raises questions about confidentiality of use of information sources, accuracy of analyses.
3. Preparing an internal marketing communication – raises questions about the best AI service to use, e.g. for visual elements, better prompting.

In all cases there is the option to say there are ethical grounds for not using AI at all.

The kind of questions your scenario might want to prompt could be:

- In what parts of the activity would it be safe and useful to use AI?
- How, if at all, would any AI use be acknowledged?
- What is the long-term impact on skills of using AI for such a task?

7

Everyday Uses of AI Chatbots in Library Work

Introduction

While the widespread adoption of AI in library services does not seem to have materialised yet, librarian and information professionals are experimenting with using its most accessible form: the AI chatbot.

In this chapter we reflect on some of the many possible uses of AI chatbots in everyday library work. We should reiterate the right to refuse to use AI chatbots, mentioned in Chapter 4. Tasks that should certainly not be given to an AI chatbot might include:

- anything that involves other people's data, including both personal data and copyrighted material
- finalising tasks, because ultimate responsibility for any output must lie with the human.

The chapter serves the purpose of showing how to put into practice some prompting principles. I have used Gemini because its available to me and as a staff member at University of Sheffield we are assured our data is not used to train the model. There are many other similar services available that would perform differently.

Everyday tasks

In our 2025 survey of CILIP members (Cox, 2025a) librarians from different sectors gave a rich range of examples of how they were exploring AI use in their practice:

- Shortening/rewriting messages for students and staff; creating minutes, summarising documents (FE librarian);
- Light-touch use of Microsoft Copilot to suggest summaries of documents and starting points for papers/presentations (National librarian);

- 'I have personally used AI to help me generate documents and come up with ideas for events' (Public librarian);
- Using AI as a tool to generate terms for search strategies and locate synonyms. Used AI to generate images for presentations and displays (HE librarian);
- 'I use AI tools primarily at the moment to trouble-shoot issues with IT systems, e.g. Microsoft Bookings, LibCal events management, Topdesk Enquiry Management System, Canvas VLE, and get step by step instructions rather than asking colleagues or logging with our IT support' (HE librarian).

The evidence seems to be that after teaching AI literacy, most librarian engagement is exploring the use of AI chatbots. There are many everyday office administrative tasks that AI chatbots can assist with (if the outputs are carefully checked):

- simple textual transformations
- transforming data from capitals to mixed case
- changing UK to American spelling
- transforming text between different formats or styles and languages, e.g. to create a presentation from a report
- drafting marketing and communications material, such as library bulletins, newsletters or e-mails
- drafting of other documentation, such as business cases or reports
- drafting and improving presentations
- drafting meeting minutes
- summarising documents or e-mail threads
- data cleaning
- planning workshop programmes and activities
- other planning, including brainstorming ideas
- drafting appraisal objectives
- making forms or writing code
- making sure text is GDPR-compliant and accessible
- translation of content.

There may be some role in processes of research and analysis:

- brainstorming search terms
- scoping research
- information on difficult-to-find subjects
- journal article summaries.

As general services, AI chatbots rarely perform satisfactorily with professional tasks:

- generating metadata on items such as books or images
- reference services – to support answering knowledge queries
- creating an alerting service based on summaries of papers
- analysing trends in access and resources borrowed.

Prompt models

In Chapter 3 I summarised the key points about prompting. It may be of interest to review some of the formalised prompt models in use (Vogel, 2024). The acronyms may help one remember key elements of a good prompt. The advice is somewhat similar.

COSTAR

COSTAR is one model of prompting:

- Context: Provide background information on the task, such as 'we are a public library in an inner-city context';
- Objective: Define the specific goal of the task, using specific terms such as summarise or list, such as 'produce a list';
- Style: Specify the desired writing style, such as 'be simple and concise';
- Tone: Set the emotional tone of the response, e.g. 'professional–formal, objective in tone' or 'educational that prompts critical questioning'. Suggest the AI adopt a particular persona for prompting;
- Audience: Define who the response is intended for, such as 'members of the general public' or '12-year-old children';
- Response: Specify the desired output format, such as how long the result should be, whether to use bullet points or output as a CSV file. Be clear about what to exclude.

AUTOMAT

Another prompting model is AUTOMAT:

- Act as – persona for chatbot to adopt, e.g. as a librarian, as a researcher;
- User persona – audience targeted;
- Targeted action – pick the verb carefully to describe what you want the AI to do, e.g. summarise or list;

- Output definition – define the type of output wanted;
- Mode – the tone of the response;
- Atypical cases – defines what the AI should do in outlier cases;
- Topic whitelisting – identify what is not to be included.

Other prompt methods

The similarities between COSTAR and AUTOMAT point to the basic principles of prompting:

- Presenting prompts in a structured form helps ensure that each element is understood.
- Chain of thought prompting – Include in the prompt a request to explain the reasoning taken in the approach so that this can be adjusted.
- Few shot prompting – give worked examples of the completed task, as opposed to zero shot prompting.
- Repeating a prompt or breaking down prompts into more than one sub-task can be helpful.
- Prompt libraries – list possible prompts to reuse.
- There are prompt sites that help you design a prompt through examples and a community who share wisdom on prompting for different generative AI platforms.

Task examples

In this section I work through some specific examples of uses in detail, seeking to assess which tasks and which aspects of tasks does AI perform well in, and how this can be improved by better prompting. All were based on Gemini and conducted in December 2025.

Converting from US English to UK English

> The patron browsed the stacks but could not find the book, so went to utilize the catalog. Still failing to find the book, they went to the circulation desk in the information center to make an inquiry.

Text I composed myself was successfully converted from US to UK English thus:

> The user browsed the shelves but could not find the book, so went to utilise the catalogue. Still failing to find the book, they went to the enquiry desk in the information centre to make an enquiry.

Gemini also explained the changes it had made.

Designing a teaching session

To test out Gemini's capabilities in designing and refining learning materials I asked the questions set out in Table 7.1. The topic chosen was explaining the environmental impact of AI. My reasoning for the wording of the prompts is given in column 2 and my evaluation of responses in the third column.

Table 7.1 *Use of Gemini in designing a teaching session*

My prompt	Thinking behind the prompt	Evaluation of the response
Give me an outline of a class to teach about the environmental impact of AI.	A very general question as a starting point.	Clearly structured plan that covers the major points around shifting attention to the material aspects of AI. Focus on data. Oriented to shifting individual behaviour. No sense of the inequalities created.
Give me the outline of one two-hour session that covers the topic of the environmental impact of AI.	I asked this to reduce the scope for closer analysis.	Timings provided.
Give me the outline of a 30-minute session to cover the topic of the environmental impact of AI.	I further reduced the time.	A usable answer with lots of ideas and tight timings. At the same time no sources to back up the facts used in the session are offered.
Give me the outline of a 30-minute session to cover the topic of the environmental impact of AI for 12-year-olds.	I added a definition of the audience.	The presentation of the ideas was shifted to be more tangible and relatable. It felt like this was a successful shift to make the same content suitable for a younger audience.
Give me the outline of a 30-minute session to cover the topic of the environmental impact of AI as part of a library AI literacy class.	I wondered if it would adjust responses to reflect a library context.	This response seemed more confused. It seemed to be targeting the general public, even though it also references university libraries.
We are an inner-city public library. We want to give a session for the public lasting 30 minutes to cover the topic of the environmental impact of AI. This will be part of a series of sessions about searching for information.	This was a second attempt to emphasise the library context.	The response still did not seem to adjust much to the library context.

Continued on next page

Table 7.1 *Continued*

My **prompt**	**Thinking behind the prompt**	**Evaluation of the response**
We are an inner-city public library. We want to give a session for the public lasting 30 minutes to cover the topic of the environmental impact of AI. This will be part of a series of sessions about searching for information, including finding books in our catalogue, using internet search, and when to use generative AI.	A further attempt to make the library context salient.	While emphasising sycophantically that 'your role as an information gatekeeper is more important than ever', there was not much sense that the library role in finding information was deemed relevant. This was the only task for which a response included a graphic. The one offered did not feel massively relevant, it was of a data centre with elements of its structure labelled.
Give me the outline of a 30-minute session to cover the topic of the environmental impact of AI as part of a library AI literacy class for university students studying humanities.	I changed the remit to be for humanities students.	I was surprised how radically different the approach offered was for humanities students. It introduced elements about the social and ecological impacts which surely were relevant in the previous sections.
Give me the outline of a 30-minute session to cover the topic of the environmental impact of AI as part of a library AI literacy class for university students studying humanities. For many of them English is their second language.	I added in an element to think about diversity in the classroom.	It incorporated ideas such as focusing on visual imagery and concrete analogies. It provided a glossary of relevant terms explained in simple English.
I have a 30-minute session to cover the topic of the environmental impact of AI as part of a library AI literacy class for university students studying humanities. I want a relatable case study that illustrates the issues, preferably set in the Global South.	I added the case study example.	It actually continued to offer an overall class with a number of case studies. The case studies were useful, but it did not seem to have exactly followed the instructions.
Would you like me to provide a one-page 'Case Study Sheet' with these facts that students can read during the session? YES.		This did not really seem to be very different from the previous classroom plan.

Continued on next page

Table 7.1 *Continued*

My **prompt**	**Thinking behind the prompt**	**Evaluation of the response**
Can you give me three references for the Uruguay Water War.	I followed up on one of the classroom plans.	It attempted to give me three different perspectives: one academic, one a more global perspective, one journalistic. Actually the first and second were both academic. The links did not seem to work from the first and the reference for the second was incomplete.
Would you like me to find a specific video or interview with the Uruguayan activists to show your students during the session? YES.	I accepted the prompt to find videos illustrating the themes in the class.	Links to three videos were given. These were very relevant and would work well as classroom links.
Would you like me to provide a 5-minute 'Reaction Activity' where students role-play as a Google executive and a local farmer based on these resources? YES.		I was particularly impressed by this because in my checklist I was intending to ask for a role-play script. It provided me with one. The text was useful in identifying keywords that each of the three stakeholders were likely to use. It was not a complete script.
Explain why 'concept matching' is relevant to teaching non-native English speakers in 100 words.	The previous answer had been premised on the claim that students need this form of teaching. I also wanted to introduce restraints on content outputs.	A clear explanation was given of the concept within the word limit.
I am teaching about the environmental impact of AI. Give me three academic resources to use.		in the past I have noticed that it could not offer academic resources. But this time it did. It explained that it had picked them on the basis of citations. Arguably the sources were a little dated, but they do exist. Two were on ArXiv, which is a good site for latest research on a topic like energy impact of AI. But it is a preprint website. The papers referenced have been formally published.

Overall, I was rather impressed with Gemini's performance:

- The planned sessions contained a lot of detail of what might be taught and would be potentially engaging.
- Each answer started by explaining what the task was, including sometimes introducing pedagogic ideas that related to how to address the target audience. This was showing that Gemini had responded to the request by putting the question in its own words.
- Each response was rapid yet rather full.
- The answers were clearly structured so they were easy to follow.
- Without prompting Gemini added useful elements. So, when a time limit was set for the class, each activity was given a timing. The objective for the teaching was given, although this had not been part of the question. For the sessions for non-native English speakers a cheat-sheet of vocabulary was provided.
- Each time Gemini offered to answer a relevant related question, generating a sense of conversation and helpfulness.

There were weaker areas:

- Unless prompted, Gemini did not offer sources for the teaching; indeed, while quoting many facts to present in the class no source was given for these. When prompted for sources these did not relate to the specific statements made. In particular, the whole teaching plan tended to be oriented around one key claim that an AI uses five times the resources compared to a standard Google search. However, there was no evidence presented to back up this claim.
- When asked for references it did not give a live link to published works, but rather tended to default to open content, including preprints.
- Given these issues, while the material was useful for ideating ideas for a class, it would take quite a lot of work to actually deliver the class, because one would need to locate relevant resources oneself.
- It shifted radically in its approach for teaching the topic to humanities students. It commented 'For university humanities students, the environmental impact of AI is best taught as a story of Environmental Justice and Extractivism' – whereas previous versions of the class had focused on making choices about careful individual use. The whole topic shifted.
- On the other hand, it did not seem to make much of an adjustment for library contexts, even when this was given emphasis in the framing of the prompt.

- Sometimes the restatement of the question was worded in a rather irritating way. For example, with the first question, the opening sentence of the response was: 'Teaching the environmental impact of AI is a timely and complex subject.' This was not relevant to the task.
- It persisted in referring to itself as 'me' as if it were a person.

Overall, I was impressed by the speed and depth of the suggestions made and most of the adjustments to different audiences. What was less impressive was the grounding in sources. This would be a significant barrier, I think, to using AI for this task beyond the generation stage, because the educator would need to access some sources to actually deliver the content.

Writing support

In this exercise I took a paper that was the basis for the section of Chapter 4 on AI's impact on the environment (published as a preprint as Cox, 2025c). I did not think it was appropriate to use someone else's content. Knowing the content of the paper in detail was helpful to evaluate the responses.

I think it is worth stating explicitly that I have never used Gemini or any chatbot in this way to support writing and in most cases I would not do so. Some of the prompts would be against publisher rules. However, having completed the experiment, in future I would consider using it to review the quality of writing in general and to consider alternative viewpoints. An analysis of the responses is shown in Table 7.2.

Table 7.2 *Use of Gemini in writing support*

My prompt	Thinking behind the prompt	Evaluation of the response
Produce an abstract for this paper.	Writing an abstract for a paper is hard and often left to the last moment, so I thought this was a good task.	Rather than producing a recognisable abstract, it produced a rather rambling summary, with bullet points (based on sub-headings) and references.
Produce a title for the paper	The existing title was just 'AI and the environment', so a new title was needed.	It produced 12 suggestions organised around four different approaches. Nearly all followed the title/subtitle format. Many used terminology that does not appear in the paper though were relevant to the theme. There was one that seemed to the point: 'The Information Professional's Guide to Framing the AI Environmental Crisis'. – although the paper does not refer to the issue as a 'crisis'.

Continued on next page

Table 7.2 *Continued*

My prompt	**Thinking behind the prompt**	**Evaluation of the response**
Would you like me to help you draft an introductory paragraph for the paper using one of these new titles? YES.	I was surprised by this offer, since the paper already had an introduction.	Again, the introduction used terms not actually referenced in the paper, notably 'deep materiality'.
Give me a 100-word abstract for the paper.	This was an attempt to get a more workable title.	This was strong in encapsulating the whole paper in 94 words. The weaker point was continuing to insert terms not used in the paper.
Produce a highlights summary in 3–5 sentences with a maximum of 85 characters each, including spaces.	Many journals use the format of highlights. Given the tight requirements this would be a very useful function.	It produced five sentences that all met the character limit requirement. Only one of the sentences would have been accurate and acceptable to use. The four others were incorrect in significant ways. However, with tweaking they could have been used.
Write a lay summary for the general public.		This was a reasonable attempt to summarise the issue of the hidden impacts of AI, but related very loosely to the actual paper.
Evaluate the paper.		Evaluate had not been defined, but Gemini stated that its evaluation would be 'based on its scholarly contribution, structure, and relevance to the field of Information Science.' It was quite interesting that it recognised that it was an IS paper, since this was not stated. The review was fairly sycophantic in stating that the paper would be a 'significant contribution to the evolving field of Critical AI Literacy.' And that 'This paper is an essential read for anyone teaching AI literacy in 2025.' As a short literature review, I think this is overstated. It also continues to attribute the term 'deep materiality' to the paper, a phrase that is not used. Also, it refers to examples taken from Uruguay, when actually the references were to the Chilean context. Only a couple of points were made of criticism.

Continued on next page

Table 7.2 *Continued*

My prompt	Thinking behind the prompt	Evaluation of the response
Critique the paper.	I was wondering how Gemini would scope critiquing compared to evaluating.	The response presented a balance of strengths and weaknesses. Its main points of critique were to focus on some areas which were much less developed, notably the potentially positive impacts of AI on science. While this was a deliberate choice in the paper, it is a reasonable point.
Critique the paper from a feminist perspective.	I gave it a more directive instruction for a perspective to critique the paper from.	This was more successful in uncovering some fundamental gaps in the approach.
Make a list of up to ten stylistic changes to the paper that would improve its readability.	The focus shifts to improving the style.	Ten suggestions were made, but many did not seem to relate to academic writing.
Make a list of up to ten stylistic changes to strengthen the paper while preserving its academic style.	The previous list seemed to make a number of suggestions that would not work for an academic paper. So, this follow-up asked it for suggestions.	The ten suggestions made were interesting and quotes from the text were used to illustrate the points. Some certainly were convincing: for example it suggested deeper signposting and stronger transitions.
Identify three stylistic changes to strengthen the paper while preserving its academic style, then correct the first four paragraphs correcting the mistakes.	In this prompt I asked Gemini to make specific changes to the text. I would regard this as an unethical and undesirable thing to do except in the context of this experiment.	I would say the writing style was significantly changed and was more forceful in its tone. At the same time, Gemini takes for granted changes that the evidence is not available to show. For example, it rewrote the opening sentences as 'The rapid integration of Artificial Intelligence (AI) into the information landscape necessitates a robust pedagogical approach to its environmental costs. As hyperscale cloud providers accelerate the construction of global data centers, the digital economy increasingly encroaches upon physical resource limits.' While this introduces the topic, part of the point of the paper is to leave openness about where the issue really lies. So, the message has been fundamentally changed in the interests of being more direct and impactful.

Continued on next page

Table 7.2 *Continued*

My prompt	Thinking behind the	Evaluation of the response
Suggest three multiple choice questions related to the paper, with answers.		The three questions did relate to the paper. While they would not test very deeply the understanding of the paper, they might be usable.
Create a graphic that adds value to the paper.	I was wondering if the paper could be enhanced by creating some sort of new visualisation.	This was a complete fail. There was a long textual answer then it offered the same graphic it had offered in the earlier activity. This scarcely related to the paper at all.
Turn the uploaded file into a 20-minute presentation with illustrative graphics.	I wanted to see how good it was at turning a text into a presentation.	It gave me the content for seven slides. Suggestions for graphics that would fit the topic of each slide were made.
Evaluate the paper [Asked in a second session].	I asked the question the next day to see if there was a different response.	The next day it gave a rather different analysis, that was actually more convincing.However, the wholly different approach taken is surprising and obviously raises questions about reproducibility.

Overall, I think Gemini's performance was quite disappointing. On the positive side:

- It generally followed instructions. Formally it could perform tasks such as meet 100-word limits. Heavily edited, the text could potentially have been made usable.
- I particularly valued the critical elements, especially the feminist analysis. The analysis could be seen as generic, but it was genuinely thought-provoking.
- The stylistic suggestions had some value. They seemed to be more than generic advice on good writing and to be applied to the paper.
- Repeating a question a few times could produce a richer set of answers.

Weaker areas of Gemini's performance:

- In summaries Gemini introduced ideas that were simply not mentioned in the paper. I think this is because it draws on a general understanding of the topic, rather than the submitted paper source.
- In rewriting it seems prone to make very large changes to texts, erasing the author's voice and shifting the argument significantly. I really recoiled

from using it in this way, since it renders one's own ideas in a garbled and unrecognisable way, quite apart from the ethical issues and publisher guidelines.

- One of the characteristics of AI chatbots is to give very full answers, rather than concise highly useful ones. There is a sense of superfluity. So, when I asked for a title a few suggestions would have been useful, to be offered 12 seems excessive. Similarly, when I asked for up to ten stylistic changes it did always give ten. Part of the strategy of satisfying the consumer is to give a very long answer quickly, rather than focus on a quality answer with a sense of priority. Of course this can be controlled at the prompt stage.
- With most responses Gemini offered a further idea for help. While creating a sense of helpfulness, I felt this was rather pressurising and some of the tasks offered were quite inappropriate. For the new user this could be very confusing.
- Given the same prompt Gemini gave different answers on different occasions. This variance partly seemed to reflect a tendency to continue thoughts from previous questions even if they were not intended to be related. Confusion between a series of tasks seems to be a source of error.

Conclusion

Even if the adoption of AI for library services has been slow, individual librarians are exploring how to use AI chatbots for useful tasks. Learning about prompting and experimenting with different tasks are necessary; they also give librarians practical understanding as the basis for training others in AI literacy. Some aspects of tasks seem to be helpful. A very simple task that can be precisely defined, such as translating a short text from American to UK English, worked well. This could be a time saving. I think in ideation of a teaching approach or in critiquing the late draft of an article AI would be extremely useful. Other uses feel far from transformational, or even damaging.

Much of the advice for prompting boils down to a few key tactics:

1. Be precise about the context, the task and the output required; also be careful about one 'conversation' infecting results in the next.
2. Iterate requests to refine answers and enable synthesising of answers, although it feels odd how different answers are at times.
3. Experiment to see in what tasks or parts of task a general AI chatbot can be useful.
4. Ask the AI chatbot to explain its reasoning. Increasingly I found this a useful default.

5 Explore different AI chatbots and be aware of rapidly changing functionality.

In addition, I would add:

6 Check the results extremely carefully and use them with caution. For example, summaries may be highly inaccurate. AI can give up on repetitive tasks without telling the user.

The last stricture does not appear in the prompting models but it is essential advice. It feels like the task of checking needs as much thought and guidance as the wording of the originating prompts. The task requires attention to detail, good fact-checking skills, and awareness of AI's usual types of error and biases. It requires pre-existing expertise. Taking time to do it carefully would be key.

Even following these simple precepts there are significant gaps in capability that reduce the value of the benefits of AI chatbots. There is probably always the need for significant human effort to manage the whole process of use, review and adapt outputs. Where accuracy is critical, one would probably hesitate to use AI except at the early ideation stage.

There is a major qualification we need to make to this commentary. We were using a generic AI chatbot to perform quite specialist tasks. It is always likely to perform less well on these than a model that has been contextually trained. This is where RAG-based systems could perform much better. Probably where Copilot is being used and has been configured with local resources the gains are greater. It is easy to imagine a service optimised for a particular context performing far better.

Activity

To enhance your own prompt skills, it would be useful to explore trying to get the AI chatbot to write a short story or a piece of flash fiction (a very short story sometimes limited to 100 words). To continue the theme, you could ask it to write a story that explores the experience of the environmental impact of AI at a human level.

Techniques you could use to develop the story through a series of prompts:

- Give a word limit to avoid very long answers and compare the outputs from different prompts.
- Start in a very open-ended way *or* give it a starting point, e.g. an opening line such as 'Jane refused to use the LLM, despite the teacher's instructions'.
- Ask it to explain its reasoning, then explicitly exclude certain logics, topics or events that you do not want to be included.

- Ask it to rewrite in a particular style: e.g. a thriller or a surreal story *or* in the style of your favourite film.
- Ask it to rewrite the story to ensure that we empathise with the main character.

In my experiments with this I was impressed by its ability to shift between genres (*Bourne Identity* to *Mary Poppins*), and word lengths, and particularly to use strategies to build up empathy with the protagonist. Ultimately, all the versions felt lacking in true originality, but they might find some place in the creative process. There are also specific tools that support creative writing.

While the potential of AI to supress our own creativity exists, there does seem to be potential to use AI to support creative writing. Ippolito et al. (2022) explored writers' hopes and uses for a writing support tool. People certainly wanted help with ideation. A number of paradigms emerged, such as: AI as a fellow writer, improvisation partner, assistant/beta reader. A number of problems were encountered, such as how to maintain control over style and the banality of many AI suggestions. Yet one feels that carefully controlled AI could be a useful writing assistant.

As an alternative you could think about simply writing your own story!

8

The Library Chatbot or Virtual Assistant

Introduction

One of the most plausible uses of AI in the library context is a library chatbot. Yet predicted widespread uses of chatbots in libraries have consistently failed to materialise. The story has evolved in rather unexpected ways. Indeed, reflecting on the chatbot 'story' tells us quite a lot about the limited truth behind technological determinism and encourages us to think about our own choices about how AI should be used.

The chatbot is a highly relatable form of AI for user interaction, unlike more difficult to understand technical applications such as machine learning. Chatbots, sometimes called 'intelligent agents' or 'conversational agents', have been defined in a number of ways, for example: 'chatbots are digital systems that can be interacted with entirely through natural language via text or voice interfaces' (Wollny et al., 2021); 'A chatbot is an intelligent agent capable of interacting with a user to answer a series of questions and provide the appropriate response' (Okonkwo & Ade-Ibijola, 2021).

Thus, chatbots are defined by their ability to communicate in conversational form, be that in text or by voice input/output. In this key aspect they can be seen as part of a wider narrative of computers imitating forms of intelligent human behaviour.

Yet the character and capabilities of chatbots have evolved over a long period and continue to evolve. It is a complex story that has been driven by technical innovation, research experiment and commercial drivers – and by practical realities and human choice. The story around the chatbot is one of the most important narratives around AI. But it is full of false starts, dead-ends and red herrings: revealing the hard-to-predict and uncontrollable nature of technology futures.

The evolution of the chatbot idea

ELIZA is often cited as the very first chatbot or chatterbot (Okonkwo & Ade-Ibijola, 2021). It was developed in the mid-1960s. It was based on pattern matching to imitate the discourse of a non-directive psychotherapist.

Leveraging a style of interaction where the therapist often echoes back to the subject in their own words produced a remarkably lifelike imitation of a real therapeutic interaction. You can still chat with a version of ELIZA at https://www.masswerk.at/elizabot/.

Other chatbot models have been based on the user picking from a series of pre-set options to get an answer to a query. This should not be considered AI but does provide a carefully controlled way to access information. The benefit is that the answers can be carefully planned, while offering the user some sense of choice. It will also be clear to the user the nature of the system they are interacting with. The limit, of course, is that pre-prepared answers may not match the user's query. While the text can be presented in an informal style, it is not going to feel like a real conversation.

From the mid-2010s there was considerable optimism or hype around chatbots; often these were based on messaging platforms and showed enhanced ability to respond in a more open-ended way to questions. The potential to use them in a wide range of ways, and for them to feel like personal assistants, was growing.

A further development in the mid 2010s was voice assistants such as Alexa, Cortana, Google home and Siri. They offered a refresh of the chatbot model based on voice communication rather than text. In many ways they mimicked good information practices by finding and citing reliable online resources when they offered answers. Labelled 'virtual assistants', they helped strengthen the idea of the chatbot as a potential helper for many tasks. As devices for the home, they increased mass familiarity with the idea of speaking to a computer and gaining an answer, as well as with gaining other services. However, after a few years voice assistants seemed to cease to be developed further. Privacy concerns were an issue, but the freezing of development was probably more to do with shifts of investment and commercial interests.

Nevertheless, towards the end of the 2010s in higher education (HE), for example, there appeared to be growing momentum to incorporate text-based chatbots for specific, local uses, such as corresponding with applicants or promoting interaction in a MOOC. For example, a 2018 report by the UK-based 'digital, data and technology agency' for tertiary education, Jisc (https://jisc.ac.uk), reflected growing confidence that HE was going to develop such chatbots for specific narrow uses at many stages of the whole learning lifecycle, including in learning (Hopkins and Maccabee, 2018). Gartner also placed chatbots as just emerging out of the 'trough of disillusionment' in its 2021 education hypecycle. They anticipated chatbots reaching the 'plateau of productivity' in two years. A key driver was seen to be that technologies from tech companies such as Google, Microsoft,

Amazon and IBM to build chatbots were becoming easier and interaction more flexible, underwritten by increasing use on customer service websites. Systematic reviews published up to 2022 continued to explore what educational uses might be important for AI chatbots (Okonkwo and Ade-Ibijola, 2021; Wollny et al., 2021).

At the same time, there remained concerns about whether people would accept working with chatbots. The ability of the technology to perform remained in question: *The Guardian* newspaper carried a fascinating story about a human being working behind the scenes to make the chatbot seem human, an example of the hidden, precarious human labour needed to make AI work (Preston, 2022). There were also a number of dramatic failures, such as Microsoft's Tay chatbot, which when opened to public use was trained by users to talk in highly inappropriate ways (Wolf et al., 2017). And in fact, the anticipated fleet of institutional chatbots across HE did not materialise.

We now know that in fact the next step of development was rather different from that anticipated. It was the launch of an LLM in chatbot form, ChatGPT in November 2022, that shifted expectations. Rather than local chatbots trained to perform narrow tasks under institutional control, the chatbot model moved towards a commercially driven AI that performed a wide range of tasks, and whose adoption was driven by users rather than institutional decision making.

The chatbot and virtual assistant ideas continue to evolve. One prediction was that 2025 would be the year of agentic AI (Paul, 2024) though this seems to have happened much slower than anticipated. Agents have been defined as: 'A category of AI systems capable of independently making decisions, interacting with their environment, and optimizing processes without direct human intervention' (Hosseini and Seilani, 2025).

Thus, agentic AI takes on complex tasks involving decision making and learning. Human control is by definition reduced; although in marketing material they are presented as assistants to a human manager (Cox, 2025b). In many ways this is a restatement of a longstanding aspiration to give computers key human attributes.

Examples, highly relevant to information work, would be the deep research features of ChatGPT and Gemini, and Copilot's Researcher and Analyst reasoning agents (Cox, 2025b). Kshetri (2025) anticipates many other uses in the educational context both in learning and administration, mostly in areas that were being predicted by Jisc nearly a decade before. In fact, writing at the end of 2025, there does not seem to have been a massive turn to agents in the HE sector: so again the AI narrative we are being told seems to be a little wrong.

Farmer, Smakman and Birtwistle (2025) see significant risks attached to the growing and unregulated use of what they call Advanced AI assistants. They speculate that an increasing way people will interact with AI is via such agents, which either give in-depth advice or act as companions and carry out tasks for people. They see significant risks in terms of privacy, skills and wellbeing.

Chatbots in the library

It is easy to see how a chatbot could be useful in a library context. Libraries do get a lot of enquires, both about how to use library services and also factual enquiries that can be answered in various ways from the collection. Chatbots could also support performing specific tasks, such as putting in a request for a particular service.

Chatbots have some obvious advantages. They can be available 24/7 unlike a human counterpart. Responses are immediate. They are potentially interactive and offer a different and so perhaps more enjoyable way to access information compared to a static web page, like a frequently asked questions document (FAQ). They should be able to respond directly to a user's questions, rather than obligating the user to formulate a search. They have the potential to be totally consistent in their answers, whereas humans might give different answers to the same question. They would be potentially free from the kind of bias that a human has in judging others who might come to ask a question face-to-face. Such consistency can be seen as advantageous, although of course human inconsistency reflects genuine differences in perception too. And, of course, chatbots could have other types of bias, such as if they struggle to understand different accents or ways of speaking because they have been trained on data without these variations.

Another major feature of AI is adaptivity or personalisation to the user's need or profile. Some forms of chatbot should be able to adapt what they offer to the individual's need.

There are also some affordances arising from the interaction with the chatbot being entirely without human involvement, such as the ability to maintain confidentiality. A study of students being asked about their accessibility needs found that they found this more acceptable than a human asking them the same question (Iniesto, Coughlan and Lister, 2021).

As a result of these potential benefits it has been predicted for some time that libraries will develop chatbots. The most obvious use is to simply field questions about the library, such as opening times and about collections. They would operate more or less as interactive FAQs.

But chatbots could be used for more specific support tasks. As an example, we can look at an educational context where a wide range of uses of chatbots in learning have been proposed, throughout the student journey (Kerly, Ellis and Bull, 2008; Tsivitanidou and Ioannou, 2020; Wellnhammer et al., 2020). They might support a user to request an interlibrary loan, by interacting with the user to gather the necessary data, rather than filling out a form. Another task would be to collect data from users, such as about their prior learning, individual learning needs or disabilities. Abbas et al. (2021) developed a chatbot to gather student evaluations of their learning in a more interactive way: this proved to increase engagement.

Chatbots might be employed to support learning, either of individual learners, or even group work, such as by prompting interaction, though encouraging constructive interaction is obviously challenging (Tegos and Demetriadis, 2017). Chatbots could have a role in creating engagement more generally, e.g. welcoming students, helping them through the transition to their course, and perhaps prompting metacognitive processes, such as reflection. They could play a similar role in engaging users with the library.

A different type of learning role is implied where chatbots act more as a companion or to offer emotional support during the learning process. The degree to which humans can develop strong relationships with chatbots is rather surprising, so perhaps this is more plausible than it might first appear (Skjuve et al., 2021). Some see a role for chatbots in supporting student well-being for this reason (Dekker et al., 2020). However, the attachments that humans are making to AI chatbots is also a cause of rising concern in the context of youth loneliness and isolation (Onside, 2025).

The AI chatbot example has also suggested the idea of animating particular collections of library material. It would be wonderful to provide a chatbot interface to a special collection, enhancing interest.

Despite these promises and a few case studies of implementations in particular institutions over a decade (e.g. Allison, 2012; Ehrenpreis and DeLooper, 2022; Rodriguez and Mune, 2022), the evidence is that there has been little development of library-designed chatbots (Guy et al., 2023). There does seem to be the beginnings of use from 2023 with services like the Springshare's chatbot embedded in LibAnswers or LibGuides being launched (Library Technology Guides, 2023). Springshare describe their chatbot as a 'rule-based, decision-tree-style answering engine', so it is not an AI solution. While simply answering queries in a structured way or directing queries to library staff they do give libraries some of the benefits of 24/7 response. Nevertheless, these tools lag far behind the latest technologies that users are experiencing in other contexts.

Issues in a library context

So, for all the potential benefits, development of library chatbots does seem to have been rather slow. How are we to explain this? Some of the explanation can be found in the capability model introduced in Chapter 5.

The resource required to create and maintain a chatbot is an obvious barrier. The technical capacities required to develop the underlying system are perhaps a key issue. Open-source solutions exist, but most libraries do not themselves develop systems.

In the past the technical resource demands might be equalled by the problem of forming and maintaining a single point of truth that addressed all relevant questions with correct answers. With an LLM-based RAG system one could upload a collection of pre-existing documents for answers to be drawn from. Though obviously one would want to iron out contradictions in the material, this is easier than assembling and maintaining a set of questions and answers.

While answering questions about the library itself or its collections is relatively straightforward, in some contexts questions can be about a substantive issue, such as to answer a factual or conceptual question. It is a lot harder to see how these can be answered from a library chatbot. It would feel critical to triage questions to a human at the right time.

Another issue could be the complexity of queries and the desire of users for human contact through their enquiries. If one examines the literature on the reference interview, while many questions may be routine, some reference questions are very complex. The presenting issue may not reflect the questioner's real need. It takes quite a sophisticated process of questioning to discover the real information need. So, it is doubtful that a chatbot could perform at this level. Fundamentally users want human contact for many questions: perhaps this is as important as answering a specific question.

Acceptability has also been a barrier. How far will different user groups find interacting with a chatbot acceptable compared to a human? In what contexts? On the one hand, the public are increasingly habituated to encountering chatbots of some form. The COVID-19 crisis accelerated familiarity with purely digital mechanisms. The success of AI chatbots may have reduced the perception of interacting with a non-human as a barrier. Indeed, asking questions of a chatbot may appeal to some user groups, such as students. It is less inhibiting than asking a potentially 'stupid question' to a human or acknowledging a disability.

However, it is not clear that a chatbot is acceptable in all circumstances. Indeed, in many commercial contexts chatbots are being used in ways that are frustrating, because it is hard to reach a human for a more complex query. Here it's clear that the use of chatbots is a cost-saving exercise, which impacts the quality of service. Maintaining the human feel of the library in many contexts such as education may be deemed a priority over efficiency of question answering. Using a LibGuide chatbot to make an FAQ more accessible might be the limit which libraries want to take.

Whatever the exact service model, from an ethical standpoint an opt-out from a chatbot is probably required. So the resource saving is qualified by the need to continue to provide answers in other forms.

The potential impact of a chatbot on librarians' work and status may also be an underlying factor. Staff resistance to the notion of creating chatbots that potentially replace them may be a key factor in discouraging managers from undertaking a resource intensive project.

Conclusion

It is fair to acknowledge that we are part-way through the chatbot story. We are being told many things about how they will evolve, such as towards agentic AI. As AI becomes more embedded in library systems, which seems to be likely, probably chatbot interfaces may spread. But we should not assume that the stories we are told about how chatbots or personal assistance will evolve are inevitable. Far from it: what we learn from reflecting on the story so far implies that we as professionals do have a say in what happens: we should be trying to write a narrative that we believe in.

The chatbot/personal assistant is an interesting ongoing story. We have seen many predictions about how this will evolve. Many predictions have been wrong: probably because they exaggerate technical possibilities or because they equate technical possibility with desirability. Librarians will want to think much more about what is useful and ethical.

Activities

Activity 1: An ethics scenario: the voice assistant

A public-facing information service has run a high-profile project to develop a voice assistant which can answer user queries. It is part of a campaign to help users understand AI better by promoting its use in a public setting. It is already proving popular and after a vote among users it has been given the name ANNA to make it as user-friendly as possible.

The voice assistant handling user enquiries promises to release hard-pressed staff to work on other duties. Furthermore, making users comfortable enough to ask sensitive questions has always been a problem at the open enquiry desk. It is thought that the public might be more willing to put sensitive questions to an impersonal chatbot and it has been located in a sound-proof booth to ensure confidentiality.

It is not all plain sailing, however.

Some frontline staff are upset and say that the voice assistant is taking away one of the most satisfying parts of their job: interacting with the public to answer their questions. They say that this contact is very important to some users who have limited other human contact. They claim that the voice assistant simply cannot replace a human in the same role. They have refused to come to any training courses about the AI. There is also a rumour that the introduction of the voice assistant was linked to the decision not to renew some contracts for weekend staff. They also claim many of the answers are inaccurate.

There is another problem: the voice assistant struggles with many accents, especially those of anyone for whom English is not their first language. Users are very diverse and many are not native English speakers. The system supplier says that it is a long-term objective to widen the range of accents (and languages) that the assistant can understand, but there is not enough demand from their wider customer base for this to be an immediate development priority.

A third issue is that some have complained that calling the virtual assistant 'ANNA' is sexist.

- What ethics and value issues do you identify?
- What would you do?

Activity 2: Design a library chatbot

Design a library AI chatbot following the prompts step by step, then reflect on the issues there could be around it.

1. What type of library do you want your chatbot to operate in?
2. What does your chatbot do? (pick one)
   - answer routine queries on the website
   - offer an introduction to the library for new users and visitors
   - gather data from users about their needs
   - answer questions about library opening hours
   - answer questions about the collections
   - allow the user to interact conversationally with a collection of material about a historical figure
   - support the user through a process such as registering for the library or requesting an interlibrary loan
   - answer library questions in an online course or MOOC
   - support group work in information literacy training
   - promote reflection during learning

- gather feedback from users after a course
- support students' wellbeing and act as a buddy
- something else – define what you think it should do.

3 What types of benefit are you imagining the chatbot will bring, and for whom? Consider these possibilities:
- cost saving
- service enhancement
- engaging face to the library
- enhanced access to knowledge
- relief for busy library staff
- enhanced user satisfaction
- improved library image.

4 Is the chatbot (a) purely text-based (b) does it have an associated avatar or visualisation? (c) is it a voice-driven agent?

5 What tone of interaction do you want to give it?
- chatty and friendly
- cool and formal
- other.

6 Does it offer predetermined choices or have an open-ended character? Does it primarily give one-off answers or is it able to have a sustained conversation (perhaps across multiple sessions)?

Reflection questions:

7 What is the probable impact on (professional and other) staff: does it replace, dominate, accelerate, divide augment, divide or enrich their work? (see Chapter 4 on ethics for a summary of these effects).

8 Do you think the chatbot raises any ethics issues, such as those of privacy or security, accuracy, bias, transparency – or other concerns?
   (a) Who will have access to data arising from interactions with chatbots and for what purposes will it be used?
   (b) How can any potential for bias be managed? Does it matter if answers are not always 100% accurate or comprehensive?
   (c) How can the working of the chatbot be adequately explained?
   (d) How is consent from the user gathered, can they opt out?
   (e) Would the chatbot be explicitly presented as non-human? If given a gender and personality, how would this be chosen? How would ground rules about acceptable behaviour towards the chatbot be established? When does the chatbot have to ask the user to consult a human member of staff?

9 What management issues does the chatbot create?

   (a) Do you think users would accept it?
   (b) Does it fit the ethos and policy of the wider organisation?
   (c) How would you evaluate its working?
   (d) How would you evaluate the ROI of the whole project of developing the chatbot?
10 Do you think it is possible technically to build this chatbot?
11 Do you think its desirable to build this chatbot?
12 Return to question 2: What is the origin of the problem that you are imagining addressing? Is this or any technology a fundamental answer to this problem?

9

AI and Library Roles in Research and Scholarly Communications

Libraries support research and scholarly communications

Libraries are a vital part of the infrastructure of research in academic institutions. National libraries are also important resources for research. AI may be beginning to reshape some of these library roles.

A key aspect of university libraries' role in research is that the search databases and collections of publications that libraries create or license are essential for researchers to understand what is already known in their subject area. Libraries often also provide literature review services. Services such as AI assistants in library-licensed databases are offering AI to support literature reviewing in new ways. This space is also being potentially reshaped by a new class of AI tools such as Scite, SciSpace, ResearchRabbit and Consensus, which offer novel ways of navigating the literature. Libraries are likely to advise on the use or licensing of these.

Libraries also have an important role in training researchers how to search databases and use collections effectively for literature reviewing. Thus, as new AI-based tools for literature search emerge, it is libraries that train users to understand how to use them in a responsible way. This could extend towards training researchers to consider all the issues with AI throughout research.

In addition, there are some cases where library collections are themselves the data for research:

- This is notably where special collections and archives of unique material are used for research in the humanities. Digitised and born-digital materials of this sort can support digital humanities research. Digital humanities is a field where use of machine learning is well established.
- Text and data mining (TDM) needs to be also mentioned here. This is the term usually used to refer to using AI data-mining techniques being used to analyse corpora of published outputs. The law varies internationally, but in the UK researchers have the right to access full

text of published material at scale for TDM. Libraries are likely to support such uses. Given the scale of publication in many fields, there is a growing need for TDM, though there are significant legal and organisational barriers to the development of this approach.

Libraries also have a strong interest in the status of scholarly communications, particularly because of their commitments to open access and open research more generally. Libraries are often responsible for managing an open-access repository for research outputs, like journal articles. These are used to promote and preserve the research content produced by the institution. One current concern generated by AI is that frequent web requests to repositories for training AI is leading to the over-burdening of repository servers, while at the same time authors are gaining no benefit from the harvested data.

From the role in running repositories and promoting open access it follows that libraries have a concern with the licences institutional authors accept for publishing their own work. Increasingly deals that libraries make to subscribe to content are linked to deals to support publication by avoiding having to pay article processing charges, so-called 'read and publish deals' or 'transformative agreements'. Libraries' interest and expertise in the publishing system may lead them to advise researchers on criteria of where to publish, including advice on publisher rules about the use of AI in research. They would also share the concern that a potential wave of AI-authored papers might seriously impact the integrity of science.

Libraries are also sometimes involved in running a press for open-access books. In such roles they would want to align to publisher standards about how AI can be used in writing.

Libraries have roles in research data management (RDM). Again, they support the management of data repositories, but also give advice on aspects of managing research data, such as the creation of descriptive metadata and licensing. They advocate for data sharing and reuse. Given the reliance AI has on data, it is likely that libraries could be heavily involved in services around data in the context of AI; these might include:

- how to find data in a complex information landscape
- the emphasis on the value of data sharing, openness and standards-based interoperability
- how to understand the provenance and quality of that data to determine its usefulness
- what data can be used for and what not (copyright, etc.)
- how to pick tools to do analysis
- how to store (or destroy) derived data.

Because of their skills in searching the literature, librarians might be involved in measuring the dissemination of research, using bibliometric indicators. This would lead them to digging deeper into citation analysis, potentially using AI.

Having emphasised the role of libraries as research infrastructure, it is important to acknowledge that there are other actors in this space, such as academic departments, ethics centres, IT services and research administrators. The library's role is always a collaborative one. The library role fits into this wider pattern, with significant local variation.

Generative AI and LIS research

A recent study by the Royal Society revealed the widespread use of AI across science technical and medical fields, with a concentration in 'medicine, materials science, robotics, agriculture, genetics, and computer science' (Royal Society, 2024). While the report acknowledges a number of challenges, it suggests that the combination of big data, algorithms and computing power may be leading to an 'inflection point'. AI is also beginning to be used more and more in other areas, creating new disciplinary fields such as computational social science and digital humanities. AI is also being introduced into other parts of the research infrastructure: such as by journal publishers as part of peer review, and by funders of research (Cox and Thelwall, 2025).

So, AI broadly conceived is having a wide impact across science. These developments are beyond the scope of the book to fully cover. Rather, as there is strong evidence of take-up of generative AI across all disciplines (OUP, 2024; Wiley, 2025), this section reflects on how generative AI might impact research and reflect on the implications for libraries.

Generative AI has potential uses throughout the research lifecycle, from conceiving a research idea through to writing up the results.

AI chatbots are general services aimed at a wide range of users; LLMs optimised for research purposes could be very powerful. For example, an LLM trained to write research proposals or papers could be useful. Institutions that were able to offer this would give their researchers significant advantages, so are likely to do so. Equally bespoke AI tools can also support specific tasks such as data collection or data analysis. Imagine an AI that supported participants completing a questionnaire or had been trained specifically to perform a type of data analysis. This again could be very powerful.

Some such tools have emerged. One of these would be specific transcription tools. Also, a new class of service with generative AI characteristics has emerged in the form of services such as:

- Consensus
- Connected papers
- Research Rabbit
- Scite
- Elicit
- Semantic scholar
- SciSpace.

They are chiefly oriented towards supporting literature reviewing, such as by visualising content, summarising specific items, and in some cases composing an entire review. They are evolving rapidly and it is again not possible to fully review them here.

Equally, publishers are introducing their own AI assistants. Being more closely tied to specific content they should be far better than a general AI chatbot.

However, given that it seems from most current studies it is still ChatGPT and the like that researchers use, in this section we focus on weighing up how AI chatbots might be used in research. Most of the comments apply across research disciplines, but I am focusing my thoughts on LIS as a discipline positioned somewhere between social science and the humanities and using a range of data collection methods, such as interviewing, surveying, and bibliometric studies.

We can consider the potential uses of AI chatbots to support research through the research lifecycle: ideation, literature reviewing, data collection, processing and analysis, writing, other dissemination and research administration.

Ideation: originating research ideas and grant writing

I think the potential for AI chatbots to be used in the ideation of research is quite low. Both originating truly original and significant research ideas and writing persuasive grant proposals are highly skilled tasks requiring a great depth of specialist knowledge. Perhaps at the very early stages of gaining familiarity with a topic AI chatbots can be helpful, but most researchers are seeking to develop a deep reputation in one field through sustained engagement with the topic, so this might not be very useful to them.

Equally, writing an excellent research proposal seems to be beyond a general AI: it's a very specific skill adapted to the funder needs and priorities. This is not to say that they could not help with some aspects of the process of writing grants, such as refining the wording of part of a proposal or mapping a proposal to funder requirements (at least for presentational aspects).

Literature reviewing

AI chatbots have more significant potential in literature reviewing.

At the search stage they could assist by suggesting search terms: it is hard to come up with comprehensive keywords to search for a topic. However, search systems already have their AI features built in to support this. The real change comes as publisher databases come to have the same ability to offer conversational search like AI chatbots. Again, in terms of monitoring the literature databases already do a good job of allowing alerts to be created. AI chatbots are not particularly current.

A more promising area is in making sense of content that has been found. English is the predominant language of scholarship. To those for whom English is not their first language, translation of literature could be extremely beneficial in improving their understanding of what is already known. Equally for English speakers translating non-English material could be hugely beneficial in widening the scope of their reviews. There is some risk attached if translations are not entirely accurate.

Summarisation of individual publications also seems a powerful possibility, especially if the researcher can both gain a summary defined appropriately through a good prompt and engage with the text in a conversational way to ask critical questions. This depends a little bit on how researchers find content. If they find content outside library systems or on journal websites, they are more likely to turn to general AI chatbots because they will have downloaded a pdf of a research paper. If an item is found via a database, increasingly publisher AI tools will support analysis there. There is a risk about violation of copyright if they upload a published pdf to an AI chatbot, but the researcher interacting with it is likely to do so intelligently. The reliability of summarisations may also be in question. Researchers need to learn how to check such summaries effectively.

If translation and summarisation of individual texts seems useful, the synthesis of a body of literature, while addressing a very important challenge for researchers arising from the exponential growth of publication, feels more problematic. AI chatbots do have tools like NotebookLM that will help with the synthesis of a number of works that the researcher uploads. They also have 'deep research' tools which yield impressive results, at least based on general web resources (Cox, 2025b).

This is where new specialist AI research tools with some AI functionality built in come into their own. Exploring SciSpace while writing this book, I was quite shocked by its ability to move from a simple question to a completed literature review. The 7,000-word report it produced was coherent and brought together a significant body of literature. As an AI agent it explained each step of the process as it did it, and one had the opportunity to adjust the parameters. The output did have a number of significant problems: the scope of its search was quite unclear and it certainly over-relied on preprints. There did not seem to be an option to integrate local library content. However, it was far better in its reach across research than the deep research tools on Gemini. Knowing the topic, I found some of the most relevant items were not included in its review. Treatment was rather "flat" in the sense that it seemed to weight equally highly relevant and less relevant works. Full use requires a subscription. Nevertheless, it did produce a coherent document that contained some convincing insights.

However, while some impressive results come from such specialist tools, AI chatbots like ChatGPT probably cannot deal adequately with complexity of synthesising a large amount of complex material.

As publisher database systems develop their own native functions (based on calling LLMs but basing answers on their content) the likelihood is that researchers might prefer these tools, assuming they work well.

So, synthesis, which is at the heart of the research process, may not be affected by AI chatbots, in comparison to the impact of translation and individual item summarisation. There could be major advances where AI has access to a broader range of content.

Data collection, processing and wrangling

AI chatbots have potential in data collection and tasks such as processing quantitative data, e.g. to check for gaps, deduplicate content or standardise variables. AI is also good at writing computer code. So, if data processing involves code, AI chatbots are likely to be very helpful.

One of the most important areas of AI use might be in transcription of data such as interviews. This has always been a time-consuming task. While some argue that the process of transcription helps with the familiarisation with the data, this seems to me doubtful. Maximising time listening to interviews and reading transcriptions closely is much more useful. However, the researcher is much more likely to use a dedicated AI transcription tool like Whispr, rather than an AI chatbot.

There are also two major barriers here that get to the heart of the risks of using AI in research:

1 The ethical risk of uploading confidential data to an AI chatbot. Especially with sensitive data, most researchers would want assurances that the data was not stored and certainly not used to train the model. It would be important to gain participant consent from research participants to such use, too.

2 The risk around inaccuracy. AI chatbots often fail to complete tasks, make errors or have persistent biases. For example, transcription from some languages could be problematic.

Data analysis

In the context of qualitative research, the evidence to date suggests that AI can support deductive coding relatively well, because it can be trained with the coding scheme and data (Wen et al., 2025). It also performs moderately well with inductive coding. It has a tendency to over-code and make errors, but it could be a useful support to the data analysis process. It might well throw up ideas that the researcher had not thought of. Prompts have to be carefully designed.

Yet the risks around confidentiality and inaccuracy recur. It is also not very reproducible: it gives different answers to the same question. This can be controlled to some extent by telling it the chain of thought to use in a prompt or if one is searching via an API by setting the temperature to zero.

As coding and theme development is hard and time-consuming, and is often done by a lone researcher, using AI to support coding feels rather helpful. To some extent it could be seen as a parallel to the idea of validating coding by a second coder, a well established practice in some forms of data analysis. But ultimately it would be the researcher that would want to retain control over the final analysis.

As many researchers already use computer-assisted qualitative data analysis software, it feels more likely that the AI functionality embedded in these tools will be used rather than AI chatbots. However, AI's ability to work at scale could lead to a more fundamental change where researchers engage with larger samples of data, rather than confine their work to small-scale studies. For more quantitative research, AI may support data analysis. Again, one suspects that AI functions built into research specialist tools are more likely to be taken up.

Writing and other dissemination

There are a wide range of tasks AI chatbots might support in academic writing, in ways that would be especially useful for non-native English speakers or those who find writing particularly challenging, such as those with dyslexia.

More routine tasks such as proof-reading or checking formatting for a journal (e.g. putting references into the right format) do seem like tasks that AI chatbots would be good at. They also carry relatively little risk.

Rephrasing text at the sentence level is a key help, but there is a risk here in terms of mis-representing the researcher's idea (see the previous chapter). Also getting a general AI to write in the right style could be problematic. The researcher might well be more likely to use a specialist academic writing tool like Grammarly.

AI chatbots could also be useful in thinking how to represent results visually, so long as the researcher stays in control over the final visualisation.

Writing a concise but informative abstract is hard, so again an AI chatbot could be helpful here.

As AI chatbots seem to be good at converting between genres and formats, using AI to create a range of different dissemination outputs could be useful. These could be lay summaries for the public or educational resources based on research. But it feels like the quality of these might not be the highest: they will always require further work and development.

The risks across writing tasks are relatively low if the ideas are already well formulated by the researcher and they are very careful to check outputs. However, the writing process is inherently creative, more a process of discovery than simply a process of articulating a given idea. In all cases the researcher needs to be in control: not just checking for accuracy of detail but also ensuring that the writing is a full representation of the researcher's ideas.

Research data management

Researchers would be likely to be carrying out certain tasks of data management, such as generating metadata about shared data so that it can be found in a data repository. AI chatbots would probably be helpful with such tasks.

Another task would be anonymisation or redaction of content. It seems doubtful that one should trust an AI chatbot with such a task, as it's unclear how that data might be used. Further, with a critical task like anonymisation of data it would have to be very carefully checked by the researcher.

Research administration

We can imagine that research administration tasks such as project time management, meeting transcription, and improving communications would be assisted. These are not essential to the integrity of the research and so feel like low-risk applications. Saving time on these tasks gives the researcher more time to focus on the core research activities.

Discussion

Table 9.1 opposite summarises the way that AI chatbots might contribute to research across its lifecycle, also indicating the extent of the benefit but also the level of risk.

Table 9.1 *Uses of AI chatbots through the research lifecycle*

AI chatbot use	Benefit	Risk
Ideation: Originating research ideas	Low	Low
Ideation: Grant writing	Low	Medium
Lit review: Search	Low	Low
Lit review: Monitor	Low	Low
Lit review: Translate	High	Low
Lit review: Summarise individual publications	High	High
Lit review: Synthesise	Medium	High
Data collection: Suggest questions	Low	Low
Data processing: Transcription	High	Medium
Data processing: Cleaning and standardising data	High	Medium
Data processing: Writing computer code	High	Low
Data analysis: quantitative analysis	Medium	High
Data analysis: qualitative analysis: deductive coding	Medium	High
Data analysis: qualitative analysis: inductive coding	Medium	High
Writing: Developing ideas for a paper	Low	High
Writing: Rephrasing	High	Medium
Writing: Detection of bias	Medium	Low
Writing: Producing visualisations	High	Medium
Writing: Formatting for a journal	High	Low
Writing: Proof reading	High	Low
Writing: Abstract composition	High	Low
Dissemination: producing different types of outputs such as lay summaries, podcasts, educational material, etc.	High	Low
Research data management	Medium	High
Administration: Drafting e-mails	Medium	Low
Administration: Time management	Medium	Low
Administration: Project meeting transcription	Medium	Low

While AI in general is aiding in research, the role of AI chatbots may be quite circumscribed because they are not specialised for research tasks. While the evidence seems to be that most researchers are just using AI chatbots, in the long run issues of reliability are likely to mean the use of more specialist tools.

There are three recurrent issues across uses with AI chatbots. Firstly, research needs to be entirely accurate, so the tendency of AI chatbots to make errors and also have bias is likely to cause problems. Maintaining research integrity is critical, so if AI is used it must be very carefully monitored by the researcher. As checking is itself a new type of task, having the skills to do this effectively need to be learned. But more deeply than this, research outputs need to be true to the insights of the researcher, so controlling the precise wording of documents is vital.

Secondly, the confidentiality issue around uploading content, especially material such as data with any level of confidentiality or sensitivity, should be seen as highly problematic. Uploading content (such as published literature) someone else has created is also problematic from an intellectual property rights perspective.

Thirdly, AI chatbots do not produce replicable results. Careful prompting (or using an API) can control this issue to some extent.

Our analysis suggests that AI chatbots would be most useful for translation of texts in a literature review, summarising individual texts, some data wrangling, some writing tasks, and for producing a range of outputs from a publication, and research project administration tasks.

As general AI chatbots are not optimised for research tasks such as academic writing style, being really good at prompting to get optimal results could be critical to successful use. Specialist AI with generative AI functionality are more likely to be used for literature synthesis, transcription, data analysis, and rewriting. As publishers catch up with generative AI, more and more tools will be embedded in search platforms. So, while generative AI could have a big impact on research AI chatbots may not be the answer. They may have a role in changing expectations, but it is the specialist tools that may really change how research is done.

The benefit is most likely to be for young researchers who might have less experience with any of these tasks and are also more likely to adopt tools than those with ingrained habits of how to do research. Older researchers already have high skills in literature reviewing and writing and do not need help, or do not think they do. Various areas of doubt such as about which tools are safe to use and ethical issues will block rapid adoption.

In low-resourced research contexts AI chatbots may be used in a wider range of tasks, in the absence of access to other more specialist tools. But overall, I feel sceptical that AI chatbots will lower global inequalities in research. Researchers in the Global South still face unfair disadvantages in terms of having to write in English, for journals typically controlled by editors in the Global North, find resources to pay huge APCs, to publish in conformity with Global North paradigms of research, as well as to cope with all sorts of obstacles to conducting research, such as weaker material and human infrastructure. Ultimately it is the rich institutions in the Global North that will have access to the best AI technologies.

One important risk is that some of the discourse around AI emphasises speed and extent of publication, and short cuts to what are essentially hard, time-consuming but ultimately the most skilled and rewarding tasks of research. Paulus and Marone (2024) analyse the way that some research tasks are constructed as mundane or boring in advertising research tools, when actually they are essential tasks. This is another example, like those mentioned in Chapter 3, of the way the AI discourse is an acceleration discourse.

There is also the risk that AI undermines researcher skills, much in the way discussed in Chapter 3 where we reflected the potential for Generative AI to drive a loss of critical analysis skills. If they become dependent on data analysis tools, researchers may lose the ability to conduct a complete research project.

Unfortunately, AI uses are more likely to impact those who are under pressure to produce and see research in a highly instrumental way. This is where a risk lies that AI chatbots may be used to help accelerate the production of weak, unoriginal research at scale. In many contexts the incentives to do this are very strong and the systems like peer review designed to prevent them are already over-strained.

While time saving is useful but not really changing the nature of research, there are a couple of areas where AI might have a more profound impact. This is particularly around being able to process data at scale. More and more researchers will be using AI to code very large bodies of data. One guesses that this might be more likely to be with quantitative researchers who have more technical skills and perhaps more confidence in understanding AI, but the ability of AI to analyse textual data may also lead to changes in the scale of studies based on content analysis.

Whereas AI chatbots might have limited impact because they are generic, generative AI functionality in dedicated tools and other AI may well have a huge impact on all disciplines, including LIS. The benefits are likely to cost money, so will be unequally distributed.

The implications for libraries

There are several implications for libraries here. Licensing and promoting the use of specialist AI tools, particularly for the literature search and synthesis parts of the lifecycle, is a clear role for librarians. These could be offerings from publishers or the new types of tools mentioned above. Librarians might input to the choice of other AI services, but it is likely decision making might occur somewhere else in the organisation. From an institutional perspective, key aspects for evaluation would be:

- cost and licensing terms
- functionality, including reliability

- integration with other tools like bibliographic software
- how user uploads/prompts are handled (e.g. not used for training the model, kept secure)
- who owns outputs
- general security concerns.

The IFLA entry point (Cox and de Braesdefer, 2025) and Nogueira et al. (2025) provide more comprehensive lists of questions that could be asked of any AI application.

There is a confusing range of other AI-based tools, available free or subscription. Offering up-to-date advice for researchers on what is safe and ethical to use is another very valuable library service.

There are also ways that the library role of training researchers to search the literature will be extended:

- effective use of AI chatbots through understanding better prompting;
- with their strong commitment to information accuracy, librarians can make an important contribution to emphasising the risks to research integrity from AI chatbot use;
- raising awareness around risk of skills loss;
- because they support researchers at different research stages with advice and training, they may also have a role in promoting understanding of wider issues such as environmental impacts;
- inputting to research policy; libraries should have a say in helping to design institutional research policies for AI. This is critical to defining acceptable uses of AI and reducing anxiety around AI use.

With their interest in scholarly communication, libraries may also play a useful role in offering advice about how to meet publisher guidelines on AI use. These are currently rather confusing (Ganjavi et al., 2024). Until a consensus emerges about how AI can be used and how to report use there will be a need for advice services.

Adopting AI tools to support RDM, so that some tasks can be performed for researchers, such as accelerating metadata creation, may also be a relevant application.

Conclusion

This chapter has focused rather narrowly on the potential impact of AI chatbots on a discipline like LIS. There are areas within STM where major advances are happening through the use of AI in general. We have also focused on general AI chatbots, not the new class of AI-based software developed specifically for research or publishers' AI tools.

If we were to analyse the potential of tailored AI tools for researchers, I think there would be a stronger sense of transformational impacts. But the evidence seems to be that most researchers, if they are using AI, are using something like ChatGPT. As the dedicated research tools become better, and if they are subscribed to by institutions and as publishers catch up, there could be significant changes. It seems to me that the key pain point is analysing the literature, because of the rate of publication. AI-based research tools that support literature analysis could enhance the quality of the use of the literature and, especially, increase the use of publications not in English.

Activities

Activity 1

Below is reproduced one of my own stories from Cox (2020). Here I am trying to imagine how research support software will develop. I am not sure how futuristic I thought it was when I wrote it; now it seems quite likely.

Reflect on the story:

- Which elements I imagined have already been accomplished?
- Which are desirable, which undesirable?
- Could the scenario promote bibliojustice or help reduce language barriers?
- How might it affect global inequalities in research?

Research Management Suite™

All members of academic staff (and PhD students) have personalised AI research support on a system licensed by the university from a consortium including a major AI platform and a consortium of big publishers.

The university has subscribed to five modules, which are described in the brochure website as follows:

'**Research Assistant™** performs background searches for literature and research data in your areas of interest. It identifies relevant material, such as published literature, data sources and news, including recent conference presentations and online discussions, and summarises it for you. It works across all languages, translating material to English (or any other language) as you require. Deep pattern matching technologies reveals potentially relevant ideas in other fields of study. It also generates candidate research hypotheses, linked to relevant literature. Fully configurable, Research Assistant ™ allows you to set key parameters such as to balance up to date with well cited literature, include different methodologies, or ensure a balance of gender in authors in material collected. It can also in real time prepare text of a draft literature review, using settings you determine.'

'**Academic Writer™** is a suite of tools to support successful research publication. It offers advanced proof-reading functionality, personalised to characteristics of your home disciplinary field and institutional/departmental style guides. On the basis of an abstract or your draft It makes ranked recommendations about which journals you could publish in to maximise the reach of your dissemination and impact. Academic Writer™ automatically edits your draft paper to fit the requirements of a target journal. It anticipates review comments for a draft paper (using data from open review and historic reviewer comments from participating journals) and suggests changes in your text to anticipate these. It also assists in responding to reviewer comments by generating first-pass responses and suggested edits. Post-publication it actively amplifies your impact through social media and ultimately citation. It generates reports on your visibility and impact, benchmarked against your field.'

'**Academic Grant Writer™** promotes your grant capture. The tool analyses your papers and research plans to suggest potential research funding schemes, as well as identifying academic collaborators and commercial partners. Using past application data and locally configured templates it dynamically creates project proposal text matching an identified funder, including producing draft text for a case for support, workpackage descriptions, impact statements and justification of resources. Options for budgets are modelled, based on institutionally determined financial parameters.'

'**Academic Collaborator™** assists in identifying research partners and uses our proprietary algorithm to predict potential partners' responsiveness and productivity. It mines global research networks to identify collaborators among your "friends of friends", enabling you to maximise the potential of your personal network. Academic Collaborator™ also mines institutional and sector wide data to identify commercial partners with an interest in your research. Access our registered collaborator network for agile partnership building.'

'**Academic Mentor ™** is our premium meta analysis service. Drawing on historic career data from across the disciplines, it identifies potential career pathways to inform your choices in your research strategy. By identifying structural holes in research fields it enables you to position your own research within emerging research activity, so maximising your visibility and contribution. Mining data from funder strategy, the latest publications, preprints and news sources, it identifies emergent interdisciplinary fields, matching your research skills and interests to the complex dynamics of the changing research landscape.'

The set-up of each assistant is mediated by a personal interview with the Intelligence Design Team (based in Research Services). Training courses are run to enable academics to optimise its use.

At a strategic level the AI is recognised to give researchers at the university a competitive advantage in publication and grant applications compared to staff in other non-research intensive institutions which have limited access to the technology. Although extremely expensive it is anticipated to make a return on investment based on grant capture, staff and PhD recruitment, and reputation.

To quote a recent press release:

'By investing in Research Management Suite, the university is making a strategic investment to consolidate its research performance compared to its comparators and anticipates that in a five-year time frame it will have a significant impact on the university's position in global league tables specifically through improving grant capture, attracting staff and PhDs, and enhancing reputation.

'Professor Goode, PVC research commented: "RMS represents a step change in the institution's commitment to research and our ambition to be a global leading research institute, with a measurable impact on improving lives. It also consolidates our position in the sector globally as a research led teaching institution".'

Some academic staff are rather reluctant to use the AI. Among their complaints are the dominance of content in the system from certain publishing providers, lack of information on how the AI works and claims of poor recommendation performance.

Controversy is growing around an HR project in the university to use the AI in recruitment and in producing 'suggestive' KPIs for academic staff.

Activity 2

You might want to write your own scenario of how future research will operate.

10

Information Futures and AI

Introduction

In a context of uncertainty many library professional organisations and those that care about libraries have turned to the methods of future studies. We are always thinking about the future in our decision making. The familiar tools of strategic thinking/foresight, such as SWOT and PESTLE, look inwards to weigh up the resources of the organisation and outwards to examine the environment it is operating in. They help us define strategies to deal with expected futures. There is a tendency for the profession to have quite a circumscribed view of the future, closely shaped by institutional strategies and a narrow temporal horizon (Cox, Pinfield and Rutter, 2019).

Future studies offers ways to open up our thinking to longer-term thinking and the more fundamental societal shifts that could impact. Organisations such as IFLA, ALA, SCONUL, CILIP and others have all sought to employ the methods of futures thinking to examine the future of the profession, or at least in one geographical or sectoral context (Dorner, Campbell-Meier and Seto, 2017). For example, the CILIP (2024) study *Future Libraries* offers an incredibly detailed examination of the context for UK public libraries.

One of the classic methods of future studies is to develop scenarios representing divergent futures. Wiebe et al. (2018) offer an excellent summary of the scenario method. The CILIP study uses this model to propose four potential futures: one worse than today, an unpredictable mix of worse and better, better than today or a continuation of today's challenges. Another approach is to develop a quadrant of scenarios based on the direction of travel for two unrelated uncertainties. The scenarios are often made more concrete through developing them as short narratives: basically, this is a structured way to produce fictional narratives.

Two of the most recent such studies offer rich material for our topic.

IFLA trend report 2024, 2025

IFLA trend report (IFLA 2024; 2025a) is a series of studies examining the fundamental trends shaping the information world globally. This is a rich resource for thinking about the conditions into which AI development occurs. In the most recent report, in addition to identifying seven key trends for information, there are also a series of ten core scenarios about the future written by the report authors in the light of these trends. In addition, guests have been invited to write seven additional scenarios. Deliberately breaking out of the four-scenario format, these suggest the many future paths for the information world. Many of these are very interesting for exploring the context within which AI developments may occur. Some specifically address possible AI developments.

For example, Scenario 1 is called AI scalpers. It imagines how workplaces change with the rise of AI Call and Queue or 'Aicue' software, which handles booking and queueing. AI scalping is the way that bad actors may exploit these queueing systems to control places in the queue to book a doctor or use library services. Some can afford to pay to move up the queue. But those who are already disadvantaged are the most likely to lose out. Not all organisations can block AI scalping. This a thought-provoking story about how the digital divides are recreated and entrenched by new technologies such as AI.

Many of the scenarios imagined in the report involved AI at some level. Many are extensions of current concerns such as censorship via sensitivity reading or the impact of English-language domination of the web on smaller languages. Each scenario feels like it recognises positive and negative aspects of likely trends.

ARL/CNI AI Scenarios: AI-Influenced Futures 2024

Even more oriented towards understanding the long-term trends with AI are the ARL/CNI (2024) AI scenarios. Rooted in a large body of rich material such as a strategic context and provocateur interviews it follows the model of creating four scenarios.

The four scenarios reflect possible outcomes from two unrelated dimensions: firstly, social control – regulation of AI and, secondly, societal adaptation to AI. This produces four scenarios:

1. democratised and socially integrated AI
2. consumer-oriented AI focused on education and entertainment
3. laissez-faire AI
4. autonomous AI.

Each scenario is explained and then presented from the perspective of Gill Rutherford, a director of an imaginary research funding organisation. A vast amount of supplementary material is provided to facilitate discussion about

AI. This is again an incredibly useful resource for thinking about the likely futures with AI, although it is a US perspective, very much focused on research libraries – there is not much mention of student experience.

We might want to think of alternative narratives, such as being trapped in a global power race between two superpowers or a number of blocs with different values.

With these resources available to the reader, in this book I take a different approach.

Some found stories

So, in the rest of the chapter, I will pick up where we left off in Chapter 1, looking at some found narratives that seem to speak to the issue of library and information futures in interesting ways.

I really wanted to close the book in an open-ended way by exploring stories of AI. So, these have not been systematically collected, they are just interesting! I think reading them reinforces the rich ways people are already imagining futures. I hope they inspire the reader to be confident to imagine their own. They are not just contemporary imaginings; we want to reflect on past ones too. They could turn out to be wrong predictions but express important concerns.

They have been written in a number of contexts, sometimes as journalism, sometimes in research projects. They hopefully reinforce our sense that narrative, including fictional narrative gives us a valuable perspective on AI, and promote a playful, exploratory viewpoint.

Welcome to Google Island – (2013) by Mat Honan

The story is by Mat Honan, now editor in chief at *MIT Technology Review*, a former *Wired* columnist.

In the story the central character finds themself transported from a conference talk to a boat that drives them to an island where they meet a virtual Larry Page, the then CEO of Google. The starting point for the story was a remark Page made about setting aside part of the world for technological experiment. In the story Page is entirely naked, reflecting, the character states, a commitment to openness. Page explains to the protagonist that the island is a Google-controlled experiment away from the frustrating limits of regulation, law and democracy. Intense monitoring through fleets of sensors, including microsensors absorbed by drinking and Google spiders, give it a panopticon vision of everything on the island, and total control. Page's vision is encapsulated when he says about Google:

> For many years now, we've looked at everything you've looked at online. Everything. We know what you want, and when you want it, down to the time of day. Why wait for you to request it? And in fact, why wait for you to discover that you even want to request it? We can just serve it to you.

It is obviously a satire on the overweening ambitions of Big Tech, controlled by a few super wealthy male individuals, to surveil and control everything through data, in ways unconstrained by any laws or protections. The assumption that past data can be used to predict and control everything is alarming and strange. I think many of us would feel that data can never do this and certainly should not do so.

Vision 2: Personal data tracking supports learning – (2015) by the LACE project

Another future vision was explored as part of a Delphi Study by the LACE Visions of the Future of Learning Analytics study (Lace Project, 2015). The co-ordinator was Dai Griffiths, then a professor at the University of Bolton, UK. The project put forward a number of visions of how learning analytics might develop in the future and asked project participants to vote on the feasibility and desirability of each. In vision 2, set in 2025, personal data tracking supports learning. The vision here is:

> By 2025, sophisticated sensors can gather personal information about factors such as posture, attention, rest, stress, blood sugar, and metabolic rate. People collect this information about their activities, and feed it into programmes of their choice that provide recommendations on how to act in ways that improve their learning.

In some ways it's the same vision as Google Island, because it is about the faith attached to data. Of course, there is a huge difference, because here it is the individuals themselves that are in control and using it in a chiefly beneficent way: to improve their own learning. There are dystopian elements, in that the story goes on to suggest that some people share their data configurations as somehow ideal models for others to copy.

Interestingly, in the project participants who voted on the scenarios, while they thought it was feasible, were very ambivalent about the desirability of the scenario, with roughly equal numbers rating it not desirable, quite desirable, desirable and very desirable. Concerns expressed in comments included those around: ownership of the data, privacy and the ability of the data to predict learning, especially as it ignores other more structural environmental factors that influence one's ability to learn.

Both these stories tell us a lot about concerns about the use of data. Stories about big data have continuity with AI because AI is data-driven.

The Box (2018) by Ryan Calo

In 2018 the University of Washington brought together a number of individuals from around the world to think about the problem that AI was being developed in just a few geographical locations, with the risk of there being a monocultural AI. The purpose was to bring people together to think about what a culturally sensitive AI might be like. Through the process participants wrote short stories that captured their thought about the implications.

Here I am going to refer mostly to the story written by Professor Calo, a legal scholar and one of the organisers, based at University of Washington School of Law (Calo, 2018).

In the story the main character Joshua invents 'The Box', which digests and outputs information of all sorts. In a seemingly generous if naive effort to share the benefits of access to information Joshua sends out boxes all across the world. After a while, seeking to discover who has benefited, he finds that it has been used for many useful things, but also banned and denounced. The twist in the story is quoted here:

> What Joshua cannot see is Uma, village screwdriver in hand, taking The Box apart, marvelling at its simple complexity. The Box showed up, belonging to no one. The innards revealed themselves easily. Yet it took Uma years of questions and bus trips and books to uncover the intricacies of the underlying code.
>
> Uma, older still, professor of engineering, marvels at the machine Joshua made. She also marvels at his choices. Imagine, shipping an expensive device to the Sahara with no dust guard. Imagine, a genie without a wish list. Imagine, building a device capable of answering any question except about itself.

The story captures some important points about the aspirations of AI. The skill to produce a useful device, but the lack of transparency of how it works or thought about needing to develop adaptations for local conditions.

It feels also like there are echoes here of the one laptop per child (OLPC) experience. OLPC was a vision to solve global inequalities by simply giving children a laptop. It has been described as a charismatic technology (Ames, 2019) the epitome of the idea that technologies can solve complex social problems. In reality OLPC largely failed because there was no consideration given to the social infrastructure needed in schools to support the laptops' use.

In other stories in the collection there are other useful thoughts about making culturally appropriate and diverse AI. For example, a participant from

Rwanda reflects on the way that chatbots that directly answer questions defy local culture in that they do not reflect local expectations about how women and men should talk to each other, and the expectation for every conversation to start with a general chat before getting to answer specific questions.

Horse, Tractor, Robot (2026) by Andrew Cox

This is one of my stories in a chapter written to update my earlier scenarios. This is chiefly a positive story about the power of translational AI. I like to keep my stories short so here I reproduce the whole of the story.

So, Jo, tell me how you are getting on with your dissertation?

Well, I guess my interest was sparked by your exploration of the South African poet who works across the nine official languages of the country. Your use of the AI agent to navigate the linguistic complexity and literary influences was really inspiring. I also wanted to explore responses to the machine as you did too in global poetry. Using the agent I was following up on your references within the course corpus. But I also looked outside and I came across the contemporary Kazakh poet, Aliyev, who writes rooted in the complex history of his country with the horse, the tractor and now the robot. In doing so he fuses Kazakh, Russian, English and increasingly Chinese language and poetic traditions.

Interesting. I have heard the name, but never read anything of his. So you found the translational functions of the agent effective?

Somewhat. And it was helpful in providing clues to the forms Aliyev draws on, be that in Russian, English or Chinese poetry. I found the deeper challenge was training it to provide effective context for the poetry in the folk myths, history and everyday life of Kazakhstan. In trying to find those connections, I contacted a local reading group in Almaty: they had recorded some group discussions about Aliyev's work, including some of his texts and commentaries not even available online. But I also organised to join one of their meetings live. They were very kind. I learned so much from them.

Wonderful!

In the story a student is studying global poetry. They discover a poet writing in a multi-linguistic context. The AI supports translation, not just of the poetry, but also to understand the cultural context of its creation. It also supports direct contact with local people also interested in this poetry, enabling them to converse with them. The point of the story is to point to the depth of translation and study work needed to engage with other cultures. How far does simple translation take us?

'A day in the life of a student at the AI University' by Gargi (2024)

Gargi was a participant in one of our workshops in the project described in Cox, Grant and Cruz (forthcoming). The project explored how students thought about AI using creative writing methods. One of the prompts was for participants to write 'A day in the life of a student at the AI university'.

Maya's alarm trilled softly, not with a jarring ring, but with a melody her personal AI assistant, Sparky, had composed the night before. Sparky knew Maya preferred calm mornings.

'Good morning, Maya,' Sparky chirped. 'Today's weather is sunny. Would you like your outfit optimised for the temperature?'

Maya stretched, opening her eyes. Through sleep-blurred vision, she saw Sparky project a few outfit options onto her bedroom wall, each with the day's forecast beside it.

'Second one, please,' she murmured. Her clothes materialised from the smart closet, perfectly pressed.

Downstairs, the aroma of coffee filled the kitchen. Sparky had anticipated her craving. On the table, her breakfast plate shimmered into existence- a perfect balance of protein, carbs, and a touch of sweetness, just how she liked it.

'Your Personalised Learning Path is updated,' Sparky announced. 'Biochemistry at 10 am is focused on neurotransmitter analysis. Shall I pull up your notes and some interactive simulations?'

'Definitely!!' Maya replied, taking a sip of her coffee.

Instead of heading to a lecture hall, Maya settled into her favorite study book. Sparky projected visuals onto the walls (some topic from her biochemistry coursework). Sparky tried to challenged her with real-world scenarios, pausing to explain where current medicine fell short.

'Okay, Sparky, let's make this interesting,' Maya grinned. 'Hypothetical scenario: a patient with an unknown neurodegenerative disease. I have access to advanced gene sequencing tech. How do I design a diagnostic test?'

Sparky hummed. 'Excellent! Let us integrate your ethics course data too. Shall we discuss the implications of genetic information privacy?'

The afternoon was a whirlwind – a collaborative VR session with students across the globe to design a sustainable water filtration system, followed by a debate on the philosophical implications of AI sentience. No rigid class schedules, just learning tailored to her interests and pace.

As evening fell, Sparky suggested, 'How about some light reading on astrophysics before bed? It'll help clear your mind after today's intense sessions.'

Maya snuggled under the covers, Sparky projecting a star map above her. The gentle narration of an AI-generated documentary soothed her into sleep, her mind buzzing with new ideas. This was not just an education – it was a journey of discovery, with Sparky as her guide every step of the way.

Many of the participant stories expressed complex concerns about the role of AI, but this particular story gives us a more inspiring vision of how AI might change the learning experience. Perhaps this is how library content might be surfaced for students in the future. It is a vision very much in line with the notion of the adaptive powers of AI, always a central story in AI for Education. Yet it also perhaps expresses a level of frustration with institutionalised learning structures.

Transcending time and language: Michel Foucault's AI comeback (2023) by Kyungmee Lee

In the aftermath of the arrival of ChatGPT, Bozkurt and many co-authors wrote speculative future narratives about the impact of AI on learning from generative AI (Bozkurt et al., 2023). At the time of writing Lee was a PhD student, now she is a senior lecturer at Lancaster University and Co-Director of the Centre for Technology Enhanced Learning

Lee's story is about a PhD student who is studying Foucault. The platform, DocAI, allows them to ask a question verbally to an AI that embodies the character of Foucault in a relatable avatar. The conversational agent not only has a comprehensive knowledge base of the philosopher's works but also contemporary scholarship on it. Compare this with the clichéed vision of Omni in the Gemini generated story in Chapter 1 – it is presumably just one of many avatars for key scholars. In the story the character of the interaction reflects the intense desire for knowledge, but also a sense of isolation and the difficulties of being heard.

Foucault listens patiently to Jin until she finishes . . . she is out of breath. In human conversations, Jin would have already paused and checked if the other person was okay. More likely, she would have been interrupted even before finishing her first ten sentences. No human is that patient nowadays.

Now, it is Foucault's turn. 'You should go back to Chapter 2 of Discipline and Punish . . . the last paragraph on page 34 . . ..' Foucault reminds Jin of one of his key ideas and explains the critical social situations in which he came up with the idea to help her.

DocAI also helps translate a recently published paper from Spanish to Korean. The student then uses 'Researcher-meet-app' to discuss with other students who appear in hologrammatic form.

The story captures the potential for new ways to interact with material like literature in more conversational ways. How might the ways users interact with library content change? How would this change academic roles, such as that of the supervisor?

The story is also interesting for the stress on the patience of the AI to listen to the student and the way the app breaks down PhD study isolation. Implicit is the sense of how learning processes are improved by the rapid and patient responses of AI. How can libraries sustain a sense of community among scholars? The author also stresses the decentring of English language through the translation as a trend favourable to decolonisation of knowledge.

The Pseudo Uni (2022) by Mark Curcher

Mark Curcher is a senior lecturer in Business and Media at Tampere University, Finland. In his institutional profile he describes himself as 'Bibliophile, Pedagogical Provocateur, Educational Emigré, Scholarly Skeptic, Balzacian Curmudgeon, Critical Contrarian, Disillusioned Dreamer, Pragmatic Pessimist, Flâneur. Immersed in the Rhizome, Punk AF!'

Curcher's (2022) story is much more pessimistic than the previous two. It is one of a number of stories by scholars published in *Post Digital Science and Education* in 2022.

In the story a student submits their entirely AI-generated work, doing so cynically because they feel the education system is out of touch with her realities. She is making money, which her out-of-date teachers do not understand. The hard-pressed academic who marks the work is just as cynical. They know students are using AI, but are also playing a game to satisfy institutional KPIs. The closing paragraph summarises a cynical take on the managerialist university.

> There are no losers in this. The students get what they want, the staff made a living, the University meets all its metrics, and the Ministry of Education, Enterprise and Innovation keeps up in the international league tables for the number of graduates. Everyone is a success, their potential unlimited. A whole lot of qualifications and not a whole lot of education, but everyone in the game is a winner! Outside the sun set in the purple sky, turning it the colour of a dead TV channel.

The story nicely captures the fear of AI in education as devaluing the entire system.

I think the story is useful in redirecting attention away from the technology to the fundamental problems of education around generational divides in experience, the commodification of learning, and managerialism. AI short-circuits any value in the game: but it is one that already seems devalued by trends that seem all too familiar.

How does the notion of the library as a store of knowledge survive these pressures?

The semantic city (2019) by Andrew Iliadis

The inspiration for the book edited by Graham et al. (2019) was to respond to a paper suggesting that if cities were run more like Amazon, they would be responsive and efficient. The book collects together a series of stories from critical scholars who imagine how a city might be run along the lines of different, familiar social media platforms such as Twitter or Instagram.

I have selected one to discuss briefly here, by Iliadis, who is a US scholar based at Temple University. Iliadis imagines a city in which AI similar to Siri is implanted directly in people's brains. In the story there is immediate access to information. It relays information such as the weather. As well as being able to say exactly when a bus will pass a certain point, the AI offers interpretations of the behaviour of others. Although Roland's parents have bought it to give him a head start and other children are jealous, there are problems. They cannot afford the version without ads. The story turns on who is responsible when the child is killed trying to cross a dangerous road.

Another story of interest is the one by Claudel (2019) which imagines a city run along the lines of a publisher.

The evolution of human science (2002) by Ted Chiang

Ted Chiang is an award-winning American SF writer. Although the short story I am referencing here (Chiang, 2002) is the oldest story among those mentioned, it is also the most futuristic. In it Chiang imagines a world in which real science driving forward change is conducted by metahumans, biologically enhanced humans, not by ordinary humans. The metahumans share their research in forms that humans cannot really understand. Humans can no longer contribute new knowledge. Human scientists are reduced to studies trying to understand metahuman findings. This remains a valid activity because the metahumans may overlook some of the value of their discoveries from the perspective of mere humans.

Conclusion

Reflecting on these stories we can see some interesting themes emerging:

- the benefits of more and more immediate information;
- the power of translational tools and increased connectivity;
- the ability to have conversational or embedded access to information;
- the power of adaptivity.

Of course, there are also many problems rising to the surface:

- inequalities of access;
- lack of transparency and loss of accountability;
- the power of Big Tech;
- over-trust in data;

- loss of accountability;
- the devaluation of learning and the potential erosion of ways of doing things in knowledge institutions like universities;
- the potential for research (or any activity) to be taken out of the hands of human researchers altogether and to be conducted by enhanced humans or AI.

We have encountered many other stories in the course of the book; hopefully you have written a few of your own. They collectively give us a rich insight into human speculation about AI.

Thinking back to Chapter 2 we might want to think of how these visions reflect concerns related to a perceived crisis in information further reinforced by the problems of generative AI. We can also think back to Cave and Dihal's (2019) characterisations of dichotomies around AI, and how they might express one of those dualisms.

Activities

Activity 1: writing your own story

The final activity of the book is to prompt a process of synthesis, wherein the reader thinks about what they have learned as a whole.

I wanted this to be a book that prompts exploration of a complex topic in an open-ended way, rather than be tempted to offer simple and reductive guidelines. It is more like a resource and guide than a set of answers.

We need to think holistically about the range of impacts of AI and its potential.

We need to integrate our information concerns and the deep ethical issues.

We have to do some speculation about a future which is rather uncertain.

We need to think hard about our local geographical and sectoral context.

Staying true to the narrative approach of the whole book, I think the best way to do this is to settle down and write your own story. Writing is an inherently creative process, where often as one writes ideas emerge. So, I would counsel you to just write and trust that insights will emerge. The aim is not to write some publishable story, but to discover what you yourself think about the topic.

If you do not feel able to do this, I think you could again go to the starting points suggested at the opening of the book.

Activity 2: Supporting others to write stories

You could also consider running a workshop for colleagues to write their own AI stories. I have referred to several projects where we have done this, e.g.

Cox and Dixon (2026). I believe it will help colleagues articulate their own hopes and concerns. Combined with other forms of data, it could feed into library policy towards AI. Some tips on how to run such workshops are given in Cox and Grant (2024).

Conclusion

I have learned so much in my preparations for writing this book: through many discussions and reading more widely. I have also learned so much in the profoundly generative processes of writing. The processes of putting ideas down on the page, thinking about ordering of thought and refining the writing have all deepened my thought.

I hope you have learned a lot from reading the book. I hope you have taken time to carry through the activities, discussed your thoughts with others and started to follow up references. I also hope you have started writing yourself. If more stories and scenarios about AI and information and libraries have been written as a result of this book that would be wonderful.

In writing this book I have learned much about the multiplicity of AI in metaphors, images and stories. AI is a very interesting idea. Also, a troubling one. I have read more widely about the ethics issues of AI. I have thought more about the connections between AI and a perceived social crisis around information. I hope reading the book has prompted you to listen out for the different narratives around AI and to be more critical about them.

In preparing the book I have read more about how librarians are already adopting AI and the ways they are explaining its safe use to users. I have also discovered more about tactics libraries can adopt to increase capability. I have reflected on the alternative visions of the AI library that we might envisage and gained a deeper sense of the differences between library sectors in how they see AI. I hope what I have written has prompted you to reflect more on how AI is changing libraries in your context and helped you to form your own vision for AI in the library.

Exploring for the book I have learned how to use an AI chatbot much more effectively. I hope this has encouraged you also to experiment more with them and start using them more critically and appropriately – or even deciding not to use them at all.

I have also learned more about using stories in research. Searching for more stories for the book, I have encountered so many visions of what AI might mean. I am sure you are noticing more of these yourself and analysing the contrasts between different stories about AI.

The overall feeling I have is that AI is a rich and complex yet incomplete idea. This incompleteness is our space of opportunity. I hope the book has played a part in making you feel more confident to talk to others about AI and engage in the wider debate happening among your colleagues and in your social circle.

I hope reading the book has prompted you to read more about AI. The amount being written about AI today is vast but there are some wonderfully clever minds commentating on the AI phenomenon. I have cited many in the references. We all need to hear more from those marginalised in the mainstream narratives, too. I hope you will search these voices out.

I hope that you have been inspired to write, too: even if that is writing only for your own understanding. Writing in any form is generative and helps you discover what you think and feel. Share your writing, too.

References

Abbas, N., Pickard, T., Atwell, E. and Walker, A. (2021) University Student Surveys Using Chatbots: Artificial Intelligence Conversational Agents. In *International Conference on Human-Computer Interaction*, Springer, 155–69.

ACRL (2024) Research Libraries Guiding Principles for Artificial Intelligence, www.arl.org/resources/research-libraries-guiding-principles-for-artificial-intelligence.

ACRL (2025) AI Competencies for Academic Library Workers, www.ala.org/acrl/standards/ai.

ARL (2024) AI Scenarios: AI-influenced Futures, www.arl.org/resources/the-arl-cni-2035-scenarios-ai-influenced-futures-in-the-research-environment.

Adam, A. (2006) *Artificial Knowing: Gender and the Thinking Machine*, Routledge.

AI4LAM (2026) Artificial Intelligence for Libraries, Archives & Museums, https://ai4lam.org.

AIIM (2025) *Explore the Power of AI Agents*, (e-book), Hyland, https://info.aiim.org/explore-the-power-of-ai-agents-ebook.

Alanoca, S., Gur-Arieh, S., Zick, T. and Klyman, K. (2025) Comparing Apples to Oranges: A Taxonomy for Navigating the Global Landscape of AI Regulation. In *Proceedings of the 2025 ACM Conference on Fairness, Accountability, and Transparency*, 914–37.

Allison, D. (2012) Chatbots in the Library: Is It Time?, *Library Hi Tech*, **30** (1), 95–107, https://doi.org/10.1108/07378831211213238.

Amer, E. and Elboghdadly, T. (2024) The End of the Search Engine Era and the Rise of Generative AI: A Paradigm Shift in Information Retrieval. In *2024 International Mobile, Intelligent, and Ubiquitous Computing Conference (MIUCC)*, IEEE 374–79.

Ames, M. (2019) *The Charisma Machine*, MIT Press.

Andrews, S. (2021) *The Case Study Companion: Teaching, Learning and Writing Business Case Studies*, Routledge.

Bates, J., Kennedy, H., Medina Perea, I., Oman, S. and Pinney, L. (2024) Socially Meaningful Transparency in Data-Based Systems: Reflections and Proposals from Practice, *Journal of Documentation*, **80** (1), 54–72.

Belshaw, D. (2025) AI Literacy or AI Literacies?, https://blog.weareopen.coop/ai-literacy-or-ai-literacies.

Benabdallah, G., Kaneko, M. A. and Desjardins, A. (2023) A Notebook of Data Imaginaries. In *Proceedings of the 2023 ACM Designing Interactive Systems Conference*, 431–45.

Better Images of AI (2025) https://betterimagesofai.org/images.

Bicker, L. (2025) Poisoned Water and Scarred Hills: The Price of the Rare Earth Metals the World Buys from China, *BBC*, www.bbc.co.uk/news/resources/idt-66cdf862-5e96-4e6e-90b8-a407b597c8d9.

Blacha-Sancho, C. (2025) How is Clarivate Addressing the Environmental Impact of AI tools in Academia, Clarivate, https://clarivate.com/academia-government/blog/reducing-the-environmental-impact-of-ai-in-academia.

Blythe, M. (2017) Research Fiction: Storytelling, Plot and Design. In *Proceedings of the 2017 CHI Conference on Human Factors in Computing Systems*, 5400–11.

Blythe, M., Andersen, K., Clarke, R. and Wright, P. (2016) Anti-solutionist Strategies: Seriously Silly Design Fiction. In *Proceedings of the 2016 CHI Conference on Human Factors in Computing System*, 4968–78.

Bozkurt, A. et al. (2023) Speculative Futures on ChatGPT and Generative Artificial Intelligence (AI): A Collective Reflection from the Educational Landscape, *Asian Journal of Distance Education*, **18** (1), 53–130.

Bradshaw, K. (2012) Developing and Using Business Ethics Scenarios, Institute of Business Ethics.

Braun, R., Lehane, O. and Lizarazu, M. R. (2024) Literary Futures: Harnessing Fiction for Futures Work, *Futures*, **158**, 103348.

Calo, R. (2018) The Box. In Calo, R., Friedman, B. and Kohno, T. (eds) Telling Stories: On Culturally Responsive AI, *Tech Policy Lab*, https://techpolicylab.uw.edu/telling-stories.

Cardon, P., Fleischmann, C., Aritz, J., Logemann, M. and Heidewald, J. (2023) The Challenges and Opportunities of AI-assisted Writing: Developing AI literacy for the AI Age, *Business and Professional Communication Quarterly*, **86** (3), 257–95.

Carroll, J. (1999) Five Reasons for Scenario-Based Design. In *Proceedings of the 32nd Hawaii International Conference on System Sciences*.

Cave, S. and Dihal, K. (2019) Hopes and Fears for Intelligent Machines in Fiction and Reality, *Nature Machine Intelligence*, **1** (2), 74–8.

Cave, S. and Dihal, K. (2020) The Whiteness of AI, *Philosophy & Technology*, **33** (4), 685–703.

Cave, S. and Dihal, K. (eds.) (2023) *Imagining AI: How the World Sees Intelligent Machines*, Oxford University Press.

Cave, S., Dihal, K. and Dillon, S. (eds) (2020) *AI Narratives: A History of Imaginative Thinking about Intelligent Machines*, Oxford University Press.

Celik, A. T. and Kaya, C. (2025) Reviewing the Expansion in Design Futuring Research: Emergent Concepts Around Speculative Design and Design Fiction, *Futures*, **171**, 103615.

Challapally, A., Pease, C., Raskar, R. and Chari, P. (2025) *The GenAI Divide: State of AI in Business 2025*, https://mlq.ai/media/quarterly_decks/v0.1_State_of_AI_in_Business_2025_Report.pdf.

Chatterji, A., Cunningham, T., Deming, D. J., Hitzig, Z., Ong, C., Shan, C. Y., and Wadman, K. (2025) How people use ChatGPT. National Bureau of Economic Research. www.nber.org/papers/w34255.

Chiang, T. (2002) The Evolution of Human Knowledge. In Chiang, T., *Stories of Your Life and Others*, Picador.

Chubb, J., Reed, D. and Cowling, P. (2022) Expert Views about Missing AI Narratives: Is There an AI Story Crisis?, *AI & Society*, **39** (3), 1107–26.

CILIP (2024) Future Libraries, www.cilip.org.uk/page/future-libraries.

Clarivate (2025) The Pulse of the Library, https://clarivate.com/pulse-of-the-library.

Claudel, M. (2019) The Civic Method. In Graham, M., Kitchin, R., Mattern, S. and Shaw, J. (eds), *How to Run a City Like Amazon and Other Fables*, Meatspace Press, 446-474.

Collett, C. (2025) The Impact of Generative AI on the Novel, *Minderoo Centre for Technology and Democracy*, www.mctd.ac.uk/impact-of-generative-ai-on-the-novel.

Colon-Aguirre, M. (2015a) Knowledge Transferred Through Organizational Stories: A Typology, *Library Management*, **36** (6/7), 421–33.

Colon-Aguirre, M. (2015b) Organizational Storytelling Among Academic Reference Librarians, *portal: Libraries and the Academy*, **15** (2), 233–50.

Conrad, D. and Wiebe, S. (eds) (2022) *Educational Fabulations: Teaching and Learning for a World Yet to Come*, Springer Nature.

Corrêa, N. K. et al. (2023) Worldwide AI Ethics: A Review of 200 Guidelines and Recommendations for AI Governance, *Patterns*, **4** (10) 1–14.

Coshow, T., Gao, A., Pingree, L., Verma, A., Scheibenreif, D., Khandabattu, H. and Olliffe, G. (2024) Top Strategic Technology Trends for 2025: Agentic AI, *Gartner Group*, www.gartner.com/doc/reprints?id=1-2K8Y7LEY&ct=250212&st=sb.

Cox, A. (2020) AI and Robots in Higher Education: Eighteen Design Fictions, University of Sheffield, Dataset, https://doi.org/10.15131/shef.data.13139816.v1.

Cox, A. (2021a) Ethics Scenarios Of Artificial Intelligence for Information and Knowledge Management and Library Professionals, University of Sheffield, Dataset, https://doi.org/10.15131/shef.data.15147411.v1.

Cox, A. (2021b) Exploring the Impact of Artificial Intelligence and Robots on Higher Education Through Literature-based Design Fictions, *International Journal of Educational Technology in Higher Education*, **18** (3), https://doi.org/10.1186/s41239-020-00237-8.

Cox A. (2022) How Artificial Intelligence (AI) Might Change Academic Library Work: Applying the Theory of the Professions, *Journal of the Association for Information Science and Technology*, special issue on AI and work, https://doi.org/10.1002/asi.24635.

Cox, A. (2023b) The Ethics of AI for Information Professionals: Eight Scenarios, *Journal of the Australian Library and Information Association*, https://doi.org/10.1080/24750158.2022.2084885.

Cox, A. (2024a) Algorithmic Literacy, AI Literacy and Responsible Generative AI Literacy, *Journal of Web Librarianship*, **18** (3), 93–110.

Cox, A. (2024b) Developing a Library Strategic Response to Artificial Intelligence, *Elucidate*, https://doi.org/10.29173/elucidate847.

Cox, A. (2025a) AI and the UK Library Profession: Survey Report 2025, www.cilip.org.uk/page/AISurveyReport2025.
Cox, A. (2025b) Our Place in the Agentic AI Loop: The Value of Information Professional Competencies, *Library HiTech News*, **43** (2), 18–20.
Cox, A. (2025c) AI and the Environment, OSF Preprint, https://doi.org/10.31235/osf.io/kmuyx_v1.
Cox, A. (2026) The Shifting Narrative Around AI in Education. In Hrastinski, S. (ed.), *Education Fiction*, Routledge.
Cox, A. and de Brasdefer, M. (2025) Entry Point for Libraries and AI, IFLA, https://repository.ifla.org/items/f197f327-dc49-4743-bb57-0a373505da8b.
Cox, A. and Dixon, N. (2026) UK Librarians' Views of Chatbots: A Study Based on Fictional Scenarios, *Journal of Academic Librarianship*, **52** (2).
Cox, A. and Grant, V. (2024) The Participatory Researcher's Creative Writing Toolkit, https://sheffield.ac.uk/media/81161/download?attachment.
Cox, A. and Jimenez, A. (2025) Chatting with the Decolonized Digital Library, *Library Trends*, **73** (4), 628–44.
Cox, A. and Mazumdar, S. (2023) Defining Artificial Intelligence for Librarians, *Journal of Librarianship and Information Science*, https://doi.org/10.1177/09610006221142029.
Cox, A. and Thelwall, M. (2025) *AI for Knowledge*, CRC press.
Cox, A., Grant, V. and Cruz, N. (forthcoming) Exploring Artificial Intelligence in Education Through Creative Writing In a Participatory Research Project.
Cox, A., Pinfield, S. and Rutter, S. (2019) The Intelligent Library: Thought Leaders' Views on the Likely Impact of Artificial Intelligence on Academic Libraries, *Library Hi Tech*, **37** (3), 418–35.
Crawford, J., Allen, K. A., Pani, B. and Cowling, M. (2024) When Artificial Intelligence Substitutes Humans in Higher Education: The Cost of Loneliness, Student Success, and Retention, *Studies in Higher Education*, **49** (5), 883–97.
Crawford, K. (2021) *The Atlas of AI: Power, Politics, and the Planetary Costs of Artificial Intelligence*, Yale University Press.
Czarniawska, B. and Joerges, B. (2020). *Robotization of Work?: Answers from Popular Culture, Media and Social Sciences*, Edward Elgar Publishing.
Curcher, M. (2022) The Pseudo Uni, *Postdigital Science and Education*, **5** (3), 558–60.
Dam, R. F. and Teo, Y. S. (2025) Personas – A Simple Introduction, Interaction Design Foundation IxDF, www.interaction-design.org/literature/article/personas-why-and-how-you-should-use-them.
Dekker, I., De Jong, E. M., Schippers, M. C., Bruijn-Smolders, D., Alexiou, A. and Giesbers, B. (2020) Optimizing Students' Mental Health and Academic Performance: AI-enhanced Life Crafting, *Frontiers in Psychology*, **11**, 1063.
Denning, S. (2012) *The Springboard*, Routledge.
Dillon, S. and Schaffer-Goddard, J. (2023) What AI Researchers Read: The Role of Literature in Artificial Intelligence Research, *Interdisciplinary Science Reviews*, **48** (1), 15–42.

Dogruel, L., Masur, P. and Joeckel, S. (2022) Development and Validation of an Algorithm Literacy Scale for Internet Users, *Communication Methods and Measures*, **16** (2), 115–33.

Dorner, D., Campbell-Meier, J. and Seto, I. (2017) Making Sense of the Future of Libraries *IFLA Journal*, **43** (4), 321–34.

Dourish, P., and Bell, G. (2014) 'Resistance is Futile': Reading Science Fiction Alongside Ubiquitous Computing. *Personal and Ubiquitous Computing, 18*, 769–778.

Down, A. and Milmo, D. (2026) 'A feedback loop with no brake': how an AI doomsday report shook US markets.

The Guardian (2026) https://www.theguardian.com/technology/2026/feb/24/feedback-loop-no-brake-how-ai-doomsday-report-rattled-markets.

Duxfield, A. and Liew, C. L. (2023) Libraries in Contemporary Science Fiction Novels: Uncertain Futures or Embedded in the Fabric of Society?, *Journal of Documentation*, **79** (3), 546–66.

Ehrenpreis, M. and DeLooper, J. (2022) Implementing a Chatbot on a Library Website, *Journal of Web Librarianship*, **16** (2), 120–42.

Emerging strategy (2026) Academic AI impact: measuring the impact of AI adoption on academic library workflows. https://clarivate.com/academia-government/wp-content/uploads/sites/3/dlm_uploads/2026/02/Clarivate-and-Emerging-Strategy-Academic-AI-Impact-Study.pdf

Estampa (2024) Cartography of Generative AI, https://cartography-of-generative-ai.net.

European Commission (2020) *White Paper on Artificial Intelligence – A European Approach to Excellence and Trust*, https://ec.europa.eu/info/sites/default/files/commission-white-paper-artificial-intelligence-feb2020_en.pdf.

Farmer, H., Smakman, J. and Birtwistle, M. (2025) The dilemmas of delegation, Ada Lovelace Institute, https://www.adalovelaceinstitute.org/report/dilemmas-of-delegation.

Freeman, J. (2025) *Student Generative AI Survey 2025*, HEPI policy note 61, www.hepi.ac.uk/wp-content/uploads/2025/02/HEPI-Kortext-Student-Generative-AI-Survey-2025.pdf.

Friends of the Earth (2025) Harnessing AI for Environmental Justice, https://policy.friendsoftheearth.uk/reports/harnessing-ai-environmental-justice.

Gabriel, Y. (2000) *Storytelling in Organizations: Facts, Fictions, and Fantasies*, Oxford University Press.

Ganjavi, C., Eppler, M. B., Pekcan, A., Biedermann, B., Abreu, A., Collins, G. S. and Cacciamani, G. E. (2024) Publishers' and journals' instructions to authors on use of generative artificial intelligence in academic and scientific publishing: bibliometric analysis, *bmj*, 384.

Gehlhaus, D. and Mutis, S. (2021) *The US AI Workforce*, https://cset.georgetown.edu/wp-content/uploads/US-AI-Workforce_Brief-1.pdf.

Gerlich, M. (2025) AI Tools in Society: Impacts on Cognitive Offloading and the Future of Critical Thinking. Societies, 15(1), 6. https://doi.org/10.3390/soc15010006.

Gidiotis, I. and Hrastinski, S. (2026) Imagining the Future of Artificial Intelligence in Education: A Review of Social Science Fiction, Learning, *Media and Technology*, **51** (1), 35–47.

Good Things Foundation (2024) Developing AI Literacy with People Who Have Low or No Digital Skills, www.goodthingsfoundation.org/policy-and-research/research-and-evidence/research-2024/ai-literacy.

Google AI (2022) How AI Works in Everyday Life, www.youtube.com/watch?v=oJC8VIDSx_Q.

Google Workspace (2025) Beyond AI Optimism, https://workspace.google.com/learning/report/content/beyond-ai-optimism.

Graham, M., Kitchin, R., Mattern, S. and Shaw, J. (eds) (2019) *How to Run a City Like Amazon and Other Fables*, Meatspace Press.

Guy, H., Cox, A., Bhalla, N., Miltner, N. and Newman-Griffis, D. (2025) The fragmentation of responsible AI: Sector variation in organisational AI policies and statements of principle. https://osf.io/preprints/socarxiv/s7jhy_v1.

Guy, J., Pival, P. R., Lewis, C. J., & Groome, K. (2023) Reference Chatbots in Canadian Academic Libraries. Information Technology and Libraries, 42(4). https://doi.org/10.5860/ital.v42i4.16511.

Habib, S., Vogel, T., Anli, X. and Thorne, E. (2024) How Does Generative Artificial Intelligence Impact Student Creativity?, *Journal of Creativity*, **34** (1), 100072.

Harer, J. B. and White, L. N. (2007) Using Stories to Manage Libraries: Adapting the Springboard Story from the Private Sector for Managing Library Services, *Technical Services Quarterly*, **25** (1), 39–50.

Hawkins, A. (2025) The World Wants China's Rare Earth Elements – What is Life Like in the Cty That Produces Them?, *The Guardian*, www.theguardian.com/world/2025/jun/26/china-rare-earths-baotou-life-metallic-elements.

Hektor, A. (2001) *What's the Use: Internet and Information Behavior in Everyday Life*, Doctoral thesis, Linkoping University, http://liu.divaportal.org/smash/record.jsf?pid=diva2%3A254863&dswid=6661.

Hibbert, M., Altman, E., Shippen, T. and Wright, M. (2024) A Framework for AI Literacy, *Educause*, https://er.educause.edu/articles/2024/6/a-framework-for-ai-literacy.

Hofmann, V., Kalluri, P. R., Jurafsky, D., & King, S. (2024) AI generates covertly racist decisions about people based on their dialect. Nature, 633(8028), 147-154.

Honan, M. (2013) Welcome to Google Island, *Wired*, www.wired.com/2013/05/on-google-island.

Hopkins, P. and Maccabee, R. (2018) *Chatbots and Digital Assistants – Getting Started in FE and HE*, Jisc, https://repository.jisc.ac.uk/7125/1/chatbots_and_digital_assistants_report.pdf.

Hosseini, S., and Seilani, H. (2025) The Role of Agentic AI in Shaping a Smart Future: A Systematic Review, *Array*, 100399.

House of Lords Select Committee on AI (2018) AI in the UK: Ready, Willing and Able?, https://committees.parliament.uk/committee/376/artificial-intelligence-committee.

Hu, T., Kyrychenko, Y., Rathje, S., Collier, N., Van Der Linden, S., & Roozenbeek, J. (2025) Generative language models exhibit social identity biases. Nature Computational Science, 5(1), 65-75.

IBM (2025) 5 trends for 2026, www.ibm.com/thought-leadership/institute-business-value/report/business-trends-2026.

IFLA (2024) Trend Report, https://repository.ifla.org/items/ae4dfcc0-8def-4318-8c4c-7f0507d15609.

IFLA (2025a) Trend Report, https://repository.ifla.org/items/ae4dfcc0-8def-4318-8c4c-7f0507d15609.

IFLA (2025b) IFLA Regional Professional Priorities Survey 2025, https://repository.ifla.org/handle/20.500.14598/4467.

Iliadis, A. (2019) The Semantic City. In Graham, M., Kitchin, R., Mattern, S. and Shaw, J. (eds), *How to Run a City Like Amazon and Other Fables*, Meatspace Press, 789–871.

Iniesto, F., Coughlan, T. and Lister, K. (2021) Implementing an Accessible Conversational User Interface: Applying Feedback from University Students and Disability Support Advisors. In *Proceedings of the 18th International Web for All Conference*, 1–5.

Ippolito, D., Yuan, A., Coenen, A. and Burnam, S. (2022) Creative Writing with an AI-Powered Writing Assistant: Perspectives from Professional Writers, https://arxiv.org/abs/2211.05030.

International Energy Agency (2025) Energy and AI, www.iea.org/reports/energy-and-ai.

Jasanoff, S. (2015) Future Imperfect: Science, Technology, and the Imaginations of Modernity. In Jasanoff, S. and Kim, S-H (eds), *Dreamscapes of Modernity: Sociotechnical Imaginaries and the Fabrication of Power*, Chicago University Press, 1–33.

Jin, Z., Meng, G., Wang, X., Wang, J., Liu, C. and Zhang, J. (2025) Understanding User Prompting Behavior in Generative AI: A Component Analysis, *Proceedings of the Association for Information Science and Technology*, **62** (1), 941–45.

Jobin, A., Ienca, M. and Vayena, E. (2019) The Global Landscape of AI Ethics Guidelines, *Nature Machine Intelligence*, **1** (9), 389–99.

Jones, W. (2010) *Keeping Found Things Found: The Study and Practice of Personal Information Management*, Morgan Kaufmann.

Kara, H. (2020) Creative Research Methods: A practical guide, second edition. Policy Press.

Kerche, F. W., Zook, M., & Graham, M. (2026) The silicon gaze: A typology of biases and inequality in LLMs through the lens of place. Platforms & Society, 3.

Kerly, A., Ellis, R. and Bull, S. (2008) Conversational Agents in E-Learning. In *International Conference on Innovative Techniques and Applications of Artificial Intelligence*, Springer, 169–82.

Kirby, D. (2010) The Future is Now: Diegetic Prototypes and the Role of Popular Films in Generating Real-world Technological Development, Social Studies of Science, **40** (1), 41–70.

Köbis, N. C., Doležalová, B. and Soraperra, I. (2021) Fooled twice: People cannot detect deepfakes but think they can. Iscience, **24**(11).

Kshetri, N. (2025) Revolutionizing Higher Education: The Impact of Artificial Intelligence Agents and Agentic Artificial Intelligence on Teaching and Operations, *IT Professional*, **27** (2), 12–16, doi: 10.1109/MITP.2025.3550697.

LACE Project (2015) Vision 2: Personal Data Tracking Supports Learning –by the LACE project, https://oro.open.ac.uk/45312/1/LAK16%20LACE%20panel%20final.pdf.

Leavy, J. (2016) *Fiction as Research Practice: Short Stories, Novellas, and Novels*, Routledge.

Lee, B. C. G. (2023) The 'Collections as ML Data' Checklist for Machine Learning and Cultural Heritage, *Journal of the Association for Information Science and Technology*, **76** (2), 375–96.

Lehuedé, S. (2025) An Elemental Ethics for Artificial Intelligence: Water as Resistance Within AI's Value Chain, *AI & Society*, **40** (3), 1761–74.

Li, L. and Bertrand, M. (2025) Fostering Critical Thinkers and Future Designers: Design Fiction Pedagogy in AI Education, *Thinking Skills and Creativity*, 101962.

Library Technology Guides (2023) Springshare Announces LibAnswers Chatbot https://librarytechnology.org/pr/28515/springshare-announces-libanswers-chatbot.

LinkedIn (2025) *AI and the Global Economy: Unlocking Growth and Reshaping Work*, https://economicgraph.linkedin.com/content/dam/me/economicgraph/en-us/PDF/ai-and-the-global-economy.pdf.

Lowagie, H. (2025) AI-powered Cataloguing: A Practical Guide to Building a Cataloguing Application with Power Apps. Facet.

Luccioni, S., Gamazaychikov, B., da Costa, T. A. and Strubell, E. (2025) Misinformation by Omission: The Need for More Environmental Transparency in AI, arXiv preprint, arXiv:2506.15572.

Ma, R., Dedema, M. and Cox, A. (2026) A Dancing Bear, a Colleague, or a Sharpened Toolbox? The Cautious Adoption of Generative AI Technologies in Digital Humanities Research, *Journal of the Association for Information Science and Technology*, DOI: 10.1002/asi.70066.

Mager, A. and Katzenbach, C. (2021) Future Imaginaries in the Making and Governing of Digital Technology: Multiple, Contested, Commodified, *New Media & Society*, **23** (2), 223–36.

Mahale, N. (2025) ChatGPT Impact on Google Search Traffic: What It Means, https://writesonic.com/blog/chatgpt-impact-on-google-search-traffic

Markham, A. (2021) The Limits of the Imaginary: Challenges to Intervening in Future Speculations of Memory, Data, and Algorithms, *New Media & Society*, **23** (2), 382–405.

Marshall, H., Wilkins, K. and Bennett, L. (2025) *Story Thinking and the Real-world Applications of Sci-Fi and Fantasy Writing*, Bloomsbury.

Masley, A. (2025) Mapping the AI & Environment Debate, blog post, https://andymasley.substack.com/p/mapping-the-ai-and-environment-debate.

Maughan, T. (2015) The Dystopian Lake Filled by the World's Tech Lust, BBC, www.bbc.co.uk/future/article/20150402-the-worst-place-on-earth.

Mayor, A. (2018) *Gods and Robots: Myths, Machines, and Ancient Dreams of Technology*, Princeton University Press.

McCarthy, J. (2004) The robot and the baby. http://jmc.stanford.edu/articles/robotandbaby.html.

Mergel, I. and Schmidt, C. (eds) (2026) *AI Innovations in Public Services: The Case of National Libraries*, Springer.

Michaels, S. (2024) The Year is 2149 and . . ., *MIT Technology Review*, www.technologyreview.com/2024/08/28/1096774/sean-michaels-2149-fiction-speculation.

Microsoft (2025) *The AI Diffusion Report; Where AI is Most Used, Developed, and Built*, www.microsoft.com/en-us/research/wp-content/uploads/2025/10/Microsoft-AI-Diffusion-Report.pdf.

Microsoft Copilot Studio (2025) Microsoft Copilot Studio Documentation, https://learn.microsoft.com/en-us/microsoft-copilot-studio.

Mikalef, P. and Gupta, M. (2021) Artificial Intelligence Capability: Conceptualization, Measurement Calibration, and Empirical Study on its Impact on Organizational Creativity and Firm Performance, *Information & Management*, **58** (3), 103434.

Mirza, R. and Seale, M. (2017) Who Killed the World? White Masculinity and the Technocratic Library of the Future. In Schlesselman-Tarango, G. (ed.), *Topographies of Whiteness: Mapping Whiteness in Library and Information Science*, Library Juice Press, 171–97.

Moeller, K. J., Kanopka, K., French, J., Hook, T. and Sedighi, M. (2024) Educational Capitalisation: a Co-formational Feminist Framework for Conceptualising Investment in For-profit Education within the Racialised and Gendered Political Economy, *Globalisation, Societies and Education*, 1–15.

Morriello, R. (2024) Libri, Biblioteche e Immaginario Tecnologico: Dagli Automi all'Intelligenza Artificiale. In Morriello, R., Roncaglia, G. and Meschini, F. (eds), *Le Biblioteche nella Fantascienza: Utopie, Distopie, Intelligenze Artificiali*, Editrice Bibliografica, 17–42.

Mozur, P., Satariano, A. and Mega, E. (2025) From Mexico to Ireland, Fury Mounts Over a Global A.I. Frenzy, *New York Times*, www.nytimes.com/2025/10/20/technology/ai-data-center-backlash-mexico-ireland.html.

Mubin, O., Wadibhasme, K., Jordan, P. and Obaid, M. (2019) Reflecting on the Presence of Science Fiction Robots in Computing Literature, *ACM Transactions on Human-Robot Interaction (THRI)*, 8 (1), 1–25.

Neale, D. (2006) Showing and Telling. In Anderson, L. (ed), *Creative Writing: A Workbook with Readings*, Routledge, 127–39.

Nielsen, L. (2002) From User to Character: An Investigation into User-descriptions in Scenarios. In *Proceedings of the 4th Conference on Designing Interactive Systems:*

Processes, Practices, Methods, and Techniques, 99–104.
Nogueira, L. A., Moltubakk, S. T., Fagervik, A. and Langfeldt, I. B. (2025) Cutting Through the Noise: Assessing Tools That Employ Artificial Intelligence, *IFLA Journal*, **51** (3), 735–49.
O'Donnell, J. and Crownhard, C. (2025) We Did the Math on AI's Energy Footprint. Here's the Story You Haven't Heard, *MIT Technology Review*, www.technologyreview.com/2025/05/20/1116327/ai-energy-usage-climate-footprint-big-tech.
OECD (2024) Explanatory Memorandum on the Updated OECD Definition of an AI System, www.oecd.org/en/publications/explanatory-memorandum-on-the-updated-oecd-definition-of-an-ai-system_623da898-en.html.
OECD (2025) Empowering Learners for the Age of AI: An AI Literacy Framework for Primary and Secondary Education. (review draft), https://ailiteracyframework.org.
Ofcom (2025) The era of answer engines, https://www.ofcom.org.uk/internet-based-services/technology/the-era-of-answer-engines-generative-ais-impact-on-search-experiences-and-online-safety
Onside (2025) Generation Isolation: OnSide Youth Research 2025, https://www.onsideyouthzones.org/generationisolation/
Okonkwo, C. W. and Ade-Ibijola, A. (2021) Chatbots Applications in Education: A Systematic Review, *Computers and Education: Artificial Intelligence*, **2**, 100033.
OUP (2024) *Researchers and AI: Survey Findings*, https://fdslive.oup.com/www.oup.com/academic/pdf/Researchers-and-AI-survey-findings.pdf.
Pace, L. A., Bruno, C. and Schwarz, J. O. (2025) Personas in Scenario Building: Integrating Human-Centred Design Methods in Foresight, *Futures*, **166**, 103539.
Papyshev, G. and Yarime, M. (2023) The State's Role in Governing Artificial Intelligence: Development, Control, and Promotion Through National Strategies, *Policy Design and Practice*, **6** (1), 79–102.
Paredes, J. L., Smith, E., Druck, G. and Benson, B. (2024) More Articles are Now Created by AI than Humans, https://graphite.io/five-percent/more-articles-are-now-created-by-ai-than-humans.
Paul, K. (2024) Autonomous Agents and Profitability to Dominate AI Agenda in 2025, Executives Forecast, *Reuters*, www.reuters.com/technology/artificial-intelligence/autonomous-agents-profitability-dominate-ai-agenda-2025-executives-forecast-2024-12-12.
Paulus, T. M. and Marone, V. (2024) 'In Minutes Instead of Weeks': Discursive Constructions of Generative AI and Qualitative Data Analysis, *Qualitative Inquiry*, 10778004241250065.
Perez, C. C. (2019) *Invisible Women: Data Bias in a World Designed for Men*, Chatto & Windus.
Pew Research Center (2025) Google users are less likely to click on links when an AI summary appears in the results, https://www.pewresearch.org/short-reads/2025/07/22/google-users-are-less-likely-to-click-on-links-when-an-ai-summary-appears-in-the-results/

Phillips, R. and Kara, H. (2021) *Creative Writing for Social Research: A Practical Guide*, Policy Press.

Pinar, A. and Cox, A. (2025) An Analysis of Artificial Intelligence (AI) Capability in Libraries and Archives, *Cataloging & Classification Quarterly*, **63** (6–7), 566–99.

Poetastros (2022) Documental 1: 'El río sueña' / SECAS – DEFENSORAS DE LAS AGUAS, www.youtube.com/watch?v=hCyfPm3Eoro.

Poushter, J., Fagan, M. and Corichi, M. (2025) How People Around the World View AI, Pew Research Center, www.pewresearch.org/global/2025/10/15/how-people-around-the-world-view-ai.

Preston, L. (2022) Becoming a chatbot: my life as a real estate AI's human backup, The Guardian, https://www.theguardian.com/technology/2022/dec/13/becoming-a-chatbot-my-life-as-a-real-estate-ais-human-backup.

Public AI Network (2025) Building Public AI with Libraries, https://publicai.network/libraries.html

Rafi, M. (2024) When AI plays favourites: How algorithmic bias shapes the hiring process, The Conversation, https://theconversation.com/when-ai-plays-favourites-how-algorithmic-bias-shapes-the-hiring-process-239471.

Rapp, A. (2020) Design Fictions for Learning: A Method for Supporting Students in Reflecting on Technology in Human-Computer Interaction Courses, *Computers & Education*, **145**, 103725.

Read, M. (2024) Drowning in Slop – A Thriving Underground Economy is Clogging the Internet with AI Garbage – and It's Only Going to Get Worse, *New York Magazine*, 23 September.

Ridley, M. (2025) Human Centered Explainable Artificial Intelligence: An Annual Review of Information Science and Technology (ARIST) Paper, *Journal of the Association for Information Science and Technology*, **76** (1), 98–120.

Ritchie, H. (2025) What's the Carbon Footprint of Using ChatGPT?, blog entry, www.sustainabilitybynumbers.com/p/carbon-footprint-chatgpt.

Rodriguez, S. and Mune, C. (2022) Uncoding Library Chatbots: Deploying a New Virtual Reference Tool at the San Jose State University Library, *Reference Services Review*, **50** (3/4), 392–405, https://doi.org/10.1108/RSR-05-2022-0020.

Roe, J., Perkins, M. and Furze, L. (2025) Reflecting Reality, Amplifying Bias? Using Metaphors to Teach Critical AI Literacy. Journal of Interactive Media in Education, 2025(1).

Royal Society (2024) Science in the Age of AI: How Artificial Intelligence is Changing the Nature and Method of Scientific Research, https://royalsociety.org/news-resources/projects/science-in-the-age-of-ai.

Salvaggio, E. (2024) Challenging The Myths of Generative AI https://www.techpolicy.press/challenging-the-myths-of-generative-ai.

Sano-Franchini, J., McIntyre, M. and Fernandes, M. (2025) Refusing Generative AI in Writing Studies, https://refusinggenai.wordpress.com.

Selwyn, N., Pangrazio, L., Nemorin, S. and Perrotta, C. (2020) What Might the School of 2030 Be Like? An Exercise in Social Science Fiction, *Learning, Media and Technology*, **45** (1), 90–106.

Sharples, M. and Pérez, R. P. (2022) *Story Machines: How Computers Have Become Creative Writers*, Routledge.

Shneiderman, B. (2022) *Human-centered AI*, Oxford University Press.

Sieker, F., Tarkowski, A., Gimpel, L. and Osborne, C. (2025) *Public AI – White Paper*, Bertelsmann Stiftungwww.bertelsmann-stiftung.de/fileadmin/files/BSt/Publikationen/GrauePublikationen/Public_AI_2025.pdf.

Silic, M., Silic, D. and Kind Trüller, K. (2025) *From Shadow IT to Shadow AI – Threats, Risks and Opportunities for Organizations*, Strategic Change.

Skjuve, M., Følstad, A., Fostervold, K. I. and Brandtzaeg, P. B. (2021) My Chatbot Companion – a Study of Human-Chatbot Relationships, *International Journal of Human-Computer Studies*, **149**, 102601.

Smith, H. and Adams, C. (2024) Thinking About Using AI? Here's What You Can and (Probably) Can't Change About Its Environmental Impact, Green Web Foundation, www.thegreenwebfoundation.org/publications/report-ai-environmental-impact.

Smith, M. (2025) What Do Britons Think AI Chatbots are Good at?, Yougov, https://yougov.co.uk/technology/articles/52062-what-do-britons-think-ai-chatbots-are-good-at.

Spiegler, S., Hoda, R. and Pant, A. (2026) Images of AI: How AI Practitioners View the Impact of Artificial Intelligence on Society, Now and in the Future, *Technology in Society*, 103109, https://doi.org/10.1016/j.techsoc.2025.103109.

Stern, N. et al. (2025) Green and Intelligent: the Role of AI in the Climate Transition, *npj Climate Action*, **4** (1), 56.

Tegos, S. and Demetriadis, S. (2017) Conversational Agents Improve Peer Learning Through Building on Prior Knowledge, *Journal of Educational Technology & Society*, **20** (1), 99–111.

Thais, S. (2024) Misrepresented Technological Solutions in Imagined Futures: The Origins and Dangers of AI Hype in the Research Community. In *Proceedings of the AAAI/ACM Conference on AI, Ethics, and Society*, **7** (1), 1455–65.

Tripper, B. and Gilman, L. (2024) *Fiction as Research: A Guide to Connecting Stories and Inquiry*, Palgrave.

Tsivitanidou, O., and Ioannou, A. (2020) Users' Needs Assessment for Chatbots' Use in Higher Education. In *Central European Conference on Information and Intelligent Systems*, Faculty of Organization and Informatics Varazdin, 55–62.

Tudorie, G. (2023) Reluctant Republic: A Positive Right for Older People to Refuse AI-Based Technology, *Societies*, **13** (12), 248.

Tufnell, N. (2018) Imagining a Science-Fiction Future, CNET, https://www.cnet.com/culture/imagining-a-sci-fi-future/

Turk, V. (2023) How AI Reduces the World to Stereotypes, *Rest of World*, https://restofworld.org/2023/ai-image-stereotypes.

UKRI (2021) *Transforming our World with AI*, www.ukri.org/wp-content/uploads/2021/02/UKRI-120221-TransformingOurWorldWithAI.pdf.

UNEP (2024) Artificial Intelligence (AI) End to End: The Environmental Impact of the Full AI Life Cycle Needs to be Comprehensively Assessed, United Nations

Environment Programme, www.unep.org/resources/report/artificial-intelligence-ai-end-end-environmental-impact-full-ai-lifecycle-needs-be.

UN scientific advisory board (2026) AI deception, https://www.un.org/scientific-advisory-board/en/ai-deception.

UNESCO (2021) Recommendation on the Ethics of Artificial Intelligence, www.unesco.org/en/articles/recommendation-ethics-artificial-intelligence.

UNESCO (2022) *K-12 AI Curricula: a Mapping of Government-endorsed AI Curricula*, https://unesdoc.unesco.org/ark:/48223/pf0000380602.

UNESCO (2024) AI Competency Framework for Students, www.unesco.org/en/articles/ai-competency-framework-students.

Urquieta, C. and Dib, D. (2024) US Tech Giants are Building Dozens of Data Centers in Chile. Locals are Fighting Back, *Rest of World*, https://restofworld.org/2024/data-centers-environmental-issues.

US National Security Commission on AI (2021) Final Report, www.nscai.gov/2021-final-report.

van Es, K. and Nguyen, D. (2025) 'Your Friendly AI Assistant': The Anthropomorphic Self-representations of ChatGPT and its Implications for Imagining AI, *AI & Society*, **40** (5), 3591–603.

Vinuesa, R. et al. (2020) The Role of Artificial Intelligence in Achieving the Sustainable Development Goals, *Nature Communications*, **11** (1), 233.

Vogel, B. (2024) The Perfect Prompt: A Prompt Engineering Cheat Sheet, https://medium.com/the-generator/the-perfect-prompt-prompt-engineering-cheat-sheet-d0b9c62a2bba.

Von Stackelberg, P. and McDowell, A. (2015) What in the World? Storyworlds, Science Fiction, and Futures Studies, *Journal of Futures Studies*, **20** (2), 25–46.

Wellnhammer, N., Dolata, M., Steigler, S. and Schwabe, G. (2020) Studying with the Help of Digital Tutors: Design Aspects of Conversational Agents that Influence the Learning Process. In *Proceedings of the 53rd Hawaii International Conference on System Sciences*, https://doi.org/10.24251/HICSS.2020.019.

Wen, C., Clough, P., Paton, R. and Middleton, R. (2025) Leveraging Large Language Models for Thematic Analysis: A Case Study in the Charity Sector, *AI & Society*, **41**, 731–48, doi: 10.1007/s00146-025-02487-4.

Wiebe, K. et al. (2018) Scenario development and foresight analysis: exploring options to inform choices. Annual Review of Environment and Resources, 43(1), 545-570.

Wiley (2025) ExplanAItions 2025: the Evolution of AI in Research, www.wiley.com/en-gb/about-us/ai-resources/ai-study.

Willcocks, L. (2020) Robo-Apocalypse cancelled? Reframing the automation and future of work debate. Journal of Information Technology, 35(4), 286-302.

Wired Magazine (2025) AI of a Thousand Faces, www.wired.com/ai-issue.

Wolf, M. J., Miller, K. W. and Grodzinsky, F. S. (2017) Why We Should Have Seen That Coming: Comments on Microsoft's Tay 'Experiment,' and Wider Implications, *The ORBIT Journal*, **1** (2), 1–12.

Wollny, S., Schneider, J., Di Mitri, D., Weidlich, J., Rittberger, M. and Drachsler, H., (2021) Are We There Yet? – A Systematic Literature Review on Chatbots in Education, *Frontiers in Artificial Intelligence*, **4**.

World Economic Forum (2025) *Future of Jobs Report*, https://reports.weforum.org/docs/WEF_Future_of_Jobs_Report_2025.pdf.

Zaidi, L. (2019) Worldbuilding in Science Fiction, Foresight and Design, *Journal of Futures Studies*, **23** (4).

Zhao, X., Cox, A. and Cai, L. (2024) ChatGPT and the Digitisation of Writing, *Humanities and Social Sciences Communications*, **11** (1), 1–9.

Index